SBC11 Contract Administration Guide

How to complete the SBC contract and its administration forms

© RIBA Publishing, 2011
Published by RIBA Publishing, 15 Bonhill Street, London EC2P 2EA

ISBN 978 1 85946 410 6
Stock Code 75662

The right of David Chappell to be identified as the Editor of this Work has been asserted in accordance with the Copyright, Design and Patents Act 1988.

All rights reserved. No part of this publication may be reproduced, stored in a retrieval system, or transmitted, in any form or by any means, electronic, mechanical, photocopying, recording or otherwise, without prior permission of the copyright owner.

British Library Cataloguing in Publications Data
A catalogue record for this book is available from the British Library.

Commissioning Editor: James Thompson
Project Manager: Robert Gray
Printed and bound by Charlesworth Group, Wakefield

While every effort has been made to check the accuracy of the information given in this book, readers should always make their own checks. Neither the Authors nor the Publisher accept any responsibility for misstatements made in it or misunderstandings arising from it.

RIBA Publishing is part of RIBA Enterprises Ltd. www.ribaenterprises.com

SBC11 Contract Administration Guide

How to complete the SBC contract and its administration forms

Edited by
David Chappell

RIBA Publishing

Editor's notes

Contract conditions often require the architect to instruct, certify, notify, etc. but seldom stipulate the use of a particular document (with a few exceptions relating to sub-contracts).

As a convenient aid to sound practice, RIBA Publishing has published a range of standard administration forms for use with the main JCT contracts. These contract administration forms have been revised to take account of the wording of the 2011 editions of the forms of contract. This booklet is a compilation of those appropriate for the Standard Building Contract 2011 (SBC11), and includes worked examples of each of the forms with notes about its use, completion and issue. It also contains checklists and references to related contract documents and other publications. It is not a commentary on the form of contract, and should an explanation of the provisions contained in the form be required, readers are advised to consult a suitable text from the list of references.

All the documents referred to in this Guide are listed in the References section (page 76) and can be obtained from RIBA Bookshops:

In store: RIBA Portland Place, Design Centre Chelsea Harbour,
                The Building Centre Bookshop
Telephone: +44 (0)191 244 5557
Online: www.ribabookshops.com

This Guide has been prepared using the JCT Standard Building Contract 2011 With Quantities (SBC/Q). Where the With Approximate Quantities (SBC/AQ) and Without Quantities (SBC/XQ) versions vary, the variants are indicated in the text. Where Amendments occur in the future, readers should check the actual issue of the form of contract that they are using and if necessary adapt the guidance given.

Worked examples

The obviously fictitious contract on which the worked examples of the administration forms are based is for the construction of a new school library in the sum of £505,096.00 with a Completion Date of 17 November 2012. The parties are The Board of Governors, Cosmeston Preparatory School, Fairbridge and L & M Construction of Fairbridge. Architects Ivor Barch Associates were commissioned by the governors to design the new library and to administer the terms of the building contract: SBC11. The firm was also appointed to act as CDM Co-ordinator, and the appointed Quantity Surveyors were William Small Partnership, also of Fairbridge.

Section completion did not form part of the contract, but when the Contractor failed to complete by the original Completion Date, the Employer, by mutual agreement, took partial possession on 23 November 2012. A Non-Completion Certificate was issued when the revised Completion Date of 19 January 2013 passed, but this was in turn overtaken by a further revised Completion Date of 26 January 2013 and so was automatically cancelled. Practical completion was certified as being on 26 January 2013, and the Final Certificate was issued on 5 October 2013.

Also available from RIBA Publishing

Contract Administration Guides:
MW11 Contract Administration Guide
IC11 Contract Administration Guide
DB11 Contract Administration Guide

Contract Administration Forms:
MW11 Project Pack
SBC11 Project Pack
IC11 Project Pack
DB11 Project Pack

Detailed JCT Contract Guidance:
Guide to MW11 (Sarah Lupton, RIBA Publishing, 2011)
Guide to SBC11 (Sarah Lupton, RIBA Publishing, 2011)
Guide to IC11 (Sarah Lupton, RIBA Publishing, 2011)
Guide to DB11 (Sarah Lupton, RIBA Publishing, 2011)

Contents

Introduction	4
Preparing and completing the form of contract	**5**
Recitals	6
Articles	10
Contract Particulars	16
The contract administration forms	**35**
Clerk of Works Direction	36
Architect's/Contract Administrator's Instruction	38
Interim Certificate	44
Statement of Retention	48
Statement of Reimbursement	50
Notice of Partial Possession by the Employer	52
Notification of Extension of Time	54
Non-Completion Certificate	58
Practical Completion Certificate	60
Section Completion Certificate	62
Certificate of Making Good	64
Final Certificate	66
Checklists and References	**69**
1: Action reminders at pre-contract stage	69
2: Architect's duties and empowered discretionary actions during work on site	71
References	76

Introduction

The Joint Contracts Tribunal has prepared the Standard Building Contract 2011 (SBC11) for major building work which follows the traditional method of procurement. The contractor is responsible for carrying out the work, and design is substantially in the hands of the architect. The employer can require the contractor to tender a lump sum price, or give an indication only of price at tender stage with the work remeasured as executed and priced on the basis of rates set out in bills of approximate quantities.

The form is suitable for use by the private sector or by local authorities either with quantities, with approximate quantities, or without quantities.

The contract can be used either where it is desired to carry out the Works as a whole or in Sections, by simply completing the relevant parts of the Contract Particulars to take account of different dates for possession and completion, different Rectification Periods and for different amounts of liquidated damages. There is also provision for the contractor to be liable for and to design part of the Works (the Contractor's Designed Portion) if so required, by reference to the Recitals and insertions in the Contract Particulars. Provision for fluctuations is included in the form of a Schedule, and consists of three options: A – Contribution, levy and tax fluctuations; B – Labour and materials cost and tax fluctuations; C – Formula adjustment.

There is no provision for nominating sub-contractors or suppliers as there was under JCT 98. If it is desired to use specialist sub-contractors for part of the work, clause 3.8 permits the insertion of a list of at least three persons in the Contract Bills from which the contractor may choose. An alternative would be for the employer to use directly employed persons under the provisions of clause 2.7. There are drawbacks to both approaches, and the relative clauses should be carefully studied.

The employer is required to appoint an architect/contract administrator, a quantity surveyor, and, where all the CDM Regulations apply, a CDM Co-ordinator, and a principal contractor. The procedures for this contract require the continued presence of such persons.

The contract does not stipulate the use of particular administration forms. However, RIBA Publishing publishes forms for use with SBC11 and worked examples of these are included in this booklet.

The contract states that each certificate shall be issued to the employer and to the contractor at the same time.

The administrative procedures under SBC11 are relatively sophisticated and need to be followed very carefully.

The Joint Contracts Tribunal (JCT) have prepared a guide (SBC/G) which provides a useful overview.

# Preparing and completing the form of contract

The Agreement

The Contract Date should be entered only after both parties have signed the Contract, which should take place before the Date of Possession stated in the Contract.

The names and addresses of the parties should be entered, and these will be the addresses to which certificates, notices, etc. should be sent (note also clause 1.7). Note that if either party is a company, a company number should be inserted.

All the necessary changes and additions to the clauses for sectional completion are now incorporated into the Contract for use as required. All the necessary changes and additions to the clauses to enable the Contractor's Designed Portion (CDP) to be used are also incorporated. Those two options are activated by the appropriate Recitals and entries in the relevant parts of the Contract Particulars. Although the part of the Contract requiring completion by the user is usefully gathered together at the beginning of the document, it is essential to read the related clauses very carefully to ensure that the results of insertions or deletions are precisely what the user intends. SBC11 is, like its predecessor (SBC05), a complex document. In the case of doubt, appropriate advice should always be obtained.

Amendments

JCT contracts inevitably become subject to Amendments over time. Whenever an Amendment is published the whole form will be reprinted to incorporate the Amendment, thus obviating the difficulties associated in the past with trying to read the text of a contract with two or three Amendments attached.

Sometimes, the parties desire to carry out their own amendments to the contracts. In principle, it is not a good idea to make significant amendments to a contract such as SBC11 in which there is a great deal of interaction between clauses. If it is thought essential to make such amendments, the advice of a suitably qualified expert in this field should be obtained. On no account should the parties attempt to carry out amendments themselves. The consequences may be quite expensive.

Recitals

The Contract extract and the notes given below relate to the With Quantities version of SBC11. The Recitals in the Without Quantities and With Approximate Quantities versions differ slightly. For information, the differences, if any, are referred to in these notes, and in the interests of clarity are printed in italics.

First Recital

The nature, scope and location of the work to be undertaken should be stated accurately and succinctly, taking care to anticipate as far as is possible that any later additions to the Works will still be covered by the description entered.

Confirms that corresponding drawings and other relevant documents have been prepared on behalf of the employer, but does not indicate by whom.

(SBC/AQ refers to a reasonably accurate forecast)

Second Recital

Confirms that the Contractor has supplied the employer with one priced copy of the Contract Bills initialled or signed by the parties.

Confirms also that the Contractor has provided the Employer with a priced schedule of activities (see Contract Particulars entry and clause 4.16.1.1). Delete if not required.

(SBC/XQ and SBC/AQ do not refer to a schedule of activities in this Recital)

Third Recital

Confirms that the Contract Drawings have been signed by the parties – and requires the Contract Drawing numbers to be entered. If the space provided proves inadequate for a full entry, refer precisely to a schedule which lists titles and numbers of all Contract Drawings. This should be firmly attached or otherwise effectively incorporated.

(SBC/XQ refers to pricing by the Contractor – either A or B method, and for the latter requires a Contract Sum Analysis or Schedule of Rates from the contractor – and to the schedule of activities)

Fourth Recital

Confirms status of Employer for purposes of the Construction Industry Scheme (CIS) (i.e. as a 'contractor'/not a 'contractor') according to the appropriate Contract Particulars entry.

Fifth Recital

Confirms that the Contractor has been provided with an Information Release Schedule (see clause 2.11). Delete if not required.

Sixth Recital

Confirms the division of the Works into Sections. Delete if there are to be no Sections and there is to be only one Date of Possession and one Completion Date.

Recitals

Whereas

First the Employer wishes to have the following work carried out[2]:

Construction of New School Library

and ancillary accommodation

at Cosmeston Preparatory School

Park Street, Fairbridge ('the Works')
and has had drawings and bills of quantities prepared which show and describe the work to be done;

Second the Contractor has supplied the Employer with a fully priced copy of the bills of quantities, which for identification has been signed or initialled by or on behalf of each Party ('the Contract Bills');

and has provided the Employer with the priced schedule of activities annexed to this Contract ('the Activity Schedule')[3];

Third the drawings are ~~numbered~~/listed in Schedule of drawings

Ref: IBA/94/20/D annexed to this Contract ('the Contract Drawings') and have for identification been signed or initialled by or on behalf of each Party[4];

Fourth for the purposes of the Construction Industry Scheme (CIS) under the Finance Act 2004, the status of the Employer is, as at the Base Date, that stated in the Contract Particulars;

~~**Fifth** the Employer has provided the Contractor with a schedule ('the Information Release Schedule') which states the information the Architect/Contract Administrator will release and the time of that release[5];~~

~~**Sixth** the division of the Works into Sections is shown in the Contract Bills and/or the Contract Drawings or in such other documents as are identified in the Contract Particulars[6];~~

---

[2] State nature and location of intended works.

[3] Delete these lines if a priced Activity Schedule is not provided.
In the Activity Schedule, each activity should be priced, so that the sum of those prices equals the Contract Sum excluding Provisional Sums and the value of work for which Approximate Quantities are included in the Contract Bills.

[4] State the identifying numbers of the Contract Drawings or identify the schedule of drawings or other document listing them, which should be annexed to this Contract, and make the appropriate deletions. The drawings themselves should be signed or initialled by or on behalf of each Party.

[5] Delete the Fifth Recital if an Information Release Schedule is not provided.

[6] Delete the Sixth Recital if the Works are not divided into Sections.

Recitals

If the contractor is not required to take liability for, or carry out, any part of the design of the Works, the ninth to twelfth Recitals inclusive must be deleted. If there is to be a Contractor's Designed Portion, these Recitals must be retained and the Seventh Recital must be completed.

Seventh Recital

The Framework Agreement only applies if identified in the Contract Particulars.

Eighth Recital

The Supplemental Provisions apply only to the extent stated in the Contract Particulars.

Ninth Recital

The nature and extent of the Contractor's Designed Portion must be inserted as precisely as possible. If there is insufficient space, refer to an additional sheet which should be signed and dated by the parties and attached to the Contract.

Tenth Recital

Confirms that the Employer has supplied the Contractor with documents setting out requirements for the design and construction of the Contractor's Designed Portion (the Employer's Requirements).

Eleventh Recital

Confirms that the Contractor has supplied documents setting out proposals for the design and construction (the Contractor's Proposals) and an analysis of the relevant part of the Contract Sum (the CDP Analysis).

Twelfth Recital

Confirms that the Employer has examined the Contractor's Proposals and is satisfied that they appear to meet the Employer's Requirements. This statement is made subject to the Conditions. This extremely guarded statement does not amount to an acceptance of the Contractor's Proposals by the Employer and its purpose is unclear. In any event, what is contained in the Recitals does not overrule perfectly clear clauses in the Contract, such as those clauses which give priority to the Employer's Requirements.

Recitals

Seventh where so stated in the Contract Particulars, this Contract is supplemented by the Framework Agreement identified in those particulars;

Eighth the Supplemental Provisions identified in the Contract Particulars apply;

The Ninth to Twelfth Recitals apply only where there is a Contractor's Designed Portion

Ninth the Works include the design and construction of[7] Air Conditioning System

_____ ('the Contractor's Designed Portion');

Tenth the Employer has supplied to the Contractor documents showing and describing or otherwise stating his requirements for the design and construction of the Contractor's Designed Portion ('the Employer's Requirements');

Eleventh in response to the Employer's Requirements the Contractor has supplied to the Employer:

- documents showing and describing the Contractor's proposals for the design and construction of the Contractor's Designed Portion ('the Contractor's Proposals'); and

- an analysis of the portion of the Contract Sum relating to the Contractor's Designed Portion ('the CDP Analysis');

Twelfth the Employer has examined the Contractor's Proposals and, subject to the Conditions, is satisfied that they appear to meet the Employer's Requirements.[8] The Employer's Requirements, the Contractor's Proposals and the CDP Analysis have each for identification been signed or initialled by or on behalf of each Party and particulars of each are given in the Contract Particulars;

---

[7] State nature of work in the Contractor's Designed Portion, or delete these four Recitals if not applicable. If the space here is insufficient a separate list should be prepared, signed or initialled by or on behalf of each Party and identified here, either as a specified Annex to this Contract or by its reference number, date or other identifier.

[8] Where the Employer has accepted a divergence from his requirements in the proposals submitted by the Contractor, the divergence should be removed by amending the Employer's Requirements before the Contract is executed.

© The Joint Contracts Tribunal Limited 2011

Preparing and completing the form of contract

Articles

Article 1

The Contractor's principal obligation. Amplified in Section 2 and Clause 3.6.

Article 2

Enter the Contract Sum in words and figures. It does not include VAT.

The Contract Sum does not change. When any amounts are added to, or deducted from it, the figure becomes the adjusted Contract Sum.

(SBC/AQ does not require a sum inserting. It is to be calculated in accordance with the conditions)

Article 3

Enter the name and address of the Architect. It is generally preferable to give the name of the practice or department rather than the name of an individual. (Unless of course the appointment of an Architect in the first place was a personal one – and then there could always be difficulties should that person move on, fall sick, etc.). The word 'of' is intended to be followed by the address of the practice and the entry should not read as the name of an individual 'of' a particular firm. Should it become necessary, clause 3.5 provides that the Employer must appoint a replacement within 21 days.

The alternative designation, 'Contract Administrator', is used here and throughout the contract where the person is not entitled to use the designation 'Architect' under the Architects Act 1997.

Article 4

Enter the name and address of the Quantity Surveyor. Should it become necessary, clause 3.5 provides that the employer must appoint a replacement within 21 days.

Articles

Now it is hereby agreed as follows

Article 1: Contractor's obligations

The Contractor shall carry out and complete the Works in accordance with the Contract Documents.

Article 2: Contract Sum

The Employer shall pay the Contractor at the times and in the manner specified in the Conditions the VAT-exclusive sum of

Five Hundred and Five Thousand and

Ninety Six Pounds Only (£ 505,096 .00) ('the Contract Sum')

or such other sum as shall become payable under this Contract.

Article 3: Architect/Contract Administrator

For the purposes of this Contract the Architect/~~Contract Administrator~~ is

Ivor Barch Associates

of Prospects Drive, Fairbridge

or, if he ceases to be the Architect/~~Contract Administrator~~, such other person as the Employer shall nominate in accordance with clause 3·5 of the Conditions.

Article 4: Quantity Surveyor

For the purposes of this Contract the Quantity Surveyor[9] is

William Small Partnership

of 3 Bank Street

Fairbridge

or, if he ceases to be the Quantity Surveyor, such other person as the Employer shall nominate in accordance with clause 3·5 of the Conditions.

---

[9] If the Architect/Contract Administrator is to exercise the Quantity Surveyor's functions under the Conditions, his name should be inserted in Article 4.

Articles

Article 5

In the event that the CDM Regulations will apply, Article 5 confirms that the Architect will also act as the CDM Co-ordinator, unless the name of an independently appointed CDM Co-ordinator is entered. Architects are advised that even if they choose to fulfil both roles on the same contract, the appointments should be kept quite separate.

Article 6

Article 6 confirms that in the absence of anything to the contrary, the Contractor will be the principal contractor for the purposes of the CDM Regulations and the SWMP Regulations.

The Employer is under a duty to appoint replacements if necessary. Clause 3.24 refers.

Delete Articles 5 and 6 if the project is not notifiable under the CDM Regulations.

Article 7

Confirms the statutory right of either party to refer any dispute to adjudication. Clause 9.2 complies with Section 108 of the Housing Grants, Construction and Regeneration Act 1996, and neither this Article nor clause 9.2 should be removed or materially amended. Clause 9.2 provides that adjudication will be in accordance with Part 1 of the Schedule to The Scheme for Construction Contracts (England and Wales) Regulations 1998. It should be noted that clause 1.4.5 makes clear that reference to legislation is to legislation as amended from time to time.

The Adjudicator can be named in the Contract Particulars. Otherwise, the appointment can be by agreement between the parties or nominated by one of the nominating bodies listed in the Contract Particulars.

Article 8

Confirms that the final resolution of any dispute or difference is to be by reference to arbitration in accordance with clauses 9.3 to 9.8. Disputes which arise under the CIS or VAT cannot be referred to arbitration if legislation provides another method. Disputes about the enforcement of an Adjudicator's decision cannot be referred to arbitration.

Note that arbitration is to be conducted under the JCT 2011 edition of the Construction Industry Model Arbitration Rules (CIMAR). Arbitration will not apply unless expressly so stated in the Contract Particulars.

In the event that the parties do not agree on the name of an Arbitrator, then the appropriate deletions in the Contract Particulars will determine the appointing body.

Articles

Article 5: CDM Co-ordinator

The CDM Co-ordinator for the purposes of the CDM Regulations is the Architect/~~Contract Administrator~~

(or)[10] _____

of _____

_____

or, if he ceases to be the CDM Co-ordinator, such other person as the Employer shall appoint pursuant to regulation 14(3) of those regulations.

Article 6: Principal Contractor

The Principal Contractor for the purposes of the CDM Regulations and the SWMP Regulations is the Contractor

(or)[10] _____

of _____

_____

or, if he ceases to be the Principal Contractor, such other contractor as the Employer shall appoint pursuant to regulation 14(3) of the CDM Regulations and/or regulation 4 of the SWMP Regulations.

Article 7: Adjudication

If any dispute or difference arises under this Contract, either Party may refer it to adjudication in accordance with clause 9·2.[11]

Article 8: Arbitration

Where Article 8 applies[12], then, subject to Article 7 and the exceptions set out below, any dispute or difference between the Parties of any kind whatsoever arising out of or in connection with this Contract shall be referred to arbitration in accordance with clauses 9·3 to 9·8 and the JCT 2011 edition of the Construction Industry Model Arbitration Rules (CIMAR). The exceptions to this Article 8 are:

- any disputes or differences arising under or in respect of the Construction Industry Scheme or VAT, to the extent that legislation provides another method of resolving such disputes or differences; and

---

[10]   Insert the name of the CDM Co-ordinator only where the Architect/Contract Administrator is not to fulfil that role, and that of the Principal Contractor only if that is to be a person other than the Contractor. If the project is not notifiable under the CDM Regulations 2007 (i.e. a project which is not likely to involve more than 30 days, or 500 person days, of construction work or which is being carried out for a homeowner as a purely domestic project), delete Articles 5 and 6 in their entirety.

[11]   As to adjudication in cases where the Employer is a residential occupier within the meaning of section 106 of the Housing Grants, Construction and Regeneration Act 1996, see the Standard Building Contract Guide.

[12]   If it is intended, subject to the right of adjudication and exceptions stated in Article 8, that disputes or differences should be determined by arbitration and not by legal proceedings, the Contract Particulars **must** state that Article 8 and clauses 9·3 to 9·8 apply and the words "do not apply" **must** be deleted. If the Parties wish any dispute or difference to be determined by the courts of another jurisdiction the appropriate amendment should be made to Article 9 (see also clause 1·11 and Schedule 5 Parts 1 and 2).

© The Joint Contracts Tribunal Limited 2011

Preparing and completing the form of contract

■ Articles

Article 9

Confirms that the final resolution of any dispute or difference is to be by legal proceedings. This is the default situation if nothing is entered in the Contract Particulars.

- any disputes or differences in connection with the enforcement of any decision of an Adjudicator.

~~Article 9: Legal proceedings~~[12]

~~Subject to Article 7 and (where it applies) to Article 8, the English courts shall have jurisdiction over any dispute or difference between the Parties which arises out of or in connection with this Contract.~~

Contract Particulars

Article 1
Part 1: General

(SBC/XQ has an insertion against the Third Recital in order to indicate the Pricing Option)

Fourth Recital and clause 4.7

Delete as appropriate to show whether employer is or is not a 'contractor' under the CIS.

Sixth Recital

If Sections are to be used, insert sufficient description to identify them. If identification is to be by means of drawings or other documents, insert the relevant drawing number, etc., have them signed and dated by the parties and attach the documents to the Contract.

Seventh Recital

If the contract is supplemented by a Framework Agreement, the date, title of and parties to the Agreement must be inserted.

Eighth Recital

Delete against each paragraph to show which of the Supplemental Provisions are to apply. If no deletions are made against a paragraph, that paragraph is to apply. If 'Notification and negotiation of disputes' applies, the nominees of the Employer and the Contractor must be inserted.

Contract Particulars

*Note: An asterisk * indicates text that is to be deleted as appropriate.*

Part 1: General

Clause etc.   *Subject*

Fourth Recital and clause 4·7 — Construction Industry Scheme (CIS)

* Employer at the Base Date
  * ~~is a 'contractor'~~/is not a 'contractor' for the purposes of the CIS

Sixth Recital — Description of Sections (if any)
(If not shown or described in the Contract Drawings or Contract Bills, state the reference numbers and dates or other identifiers of documents in which they are shown.)[13]

Seventh Recital — Framework Agreement (if applicable)
(State date, title and parties.)

Eighth Recital and Schedule 8 — Supplemental Provisions
(Where neither entry against an item below is deleted, the relevant paragraph applies.)

Collaborative working — Paragraph 1
* applies/~~does not apply~~

Health and safety — Paragraph 2
* applies/~~does not apply~~

Cost savings and value improvements — Paragraph 3
* applies/~~does not apply~~

Sustainable development and environmental considerations — Paragraph 4
* applies/~~does not apply~~

Performance Indicators and monitoring — Paragraph 5
* applies/~~does not apply~~

---

[13]   If the relevant document or set of documents takes the form of an Annex to this Contract, it is sufficient to refer to that Annex.

■ Contract Particulars

Tenth Recital

If the Contractor's Designed Portion (CDP) is to be used, identify the Employer's Requirements documents, have them signed and dated by the parties and attach them to the Contract.

Eleventh Recital

If the Contractor's Designed Portion (CDP) is to be used, identify the Contractor's Proposals documents, have them signed and attach them to the Contract.

Eleventh Recital

If the Contractor's Designed Portion (CDP) is to be used, identify the CDP Analysis documents, have them signed and dated by the parties and attach to the Contract.

Article 8

Delete as appropriate to show whether arbitration is or is not to apply. If no deletion is made, arbitration will not apply.

1.1 Enter the date decided upon as the Base Date. It must be a precise date and it is referred to in many clauses including 2.17.1, 2.29.13, 4.6.1, 4.6.2, 4.22, 5.7, 6.17 and in many places in Schedules 2 and 7.

		Notification and negotiation of disputes	Paragraph 6 *applies/~~does not apply~~
		Where paragraph 6 applies, the respective nominees of the Parties are	Employer's nominee Esther Dunn Contractor's nominee Al Ovar or such replacement as each Party may notify to the other from time to time
Tenth Recital		Employer's Requirements *(State reference numbers and dates or other identifiers of documents in which these are contained.)*[13]	Document ER/1 Dated 2 May 2011 Annexed hereto
Eleventh Recital		Contractor's Proposals *(State reference numbers and dates or other identifiers of documents in which these are contained.)*[13]	Document CP/2 Dated 19 October 2011 Annexed hereto
Eleventh Recital		CDP Analysis *(State reference numbers and dates or other identifiers of documents in which this is contained.)*[13]	Document CDPA/3 Dated 21 October 2011 Annexed hereto
Article 8		Arbitration *(If neither entry is deleted, Article 8 and clauses 9·3 to 9·8 do not apply. If disputes and differences are to be determined by arbitration and not by legal proceedings, it <u>must</u> be stated that Article 8 and clauses 9·3 to 9·8 apply.)*[14]	Article 8 and clauses 9·3 to 9·8 (*Arbitration*) *apply/~~do not apply~~
1·1		Base Date	28 November 2011

[14] On factors to be taken into account by the Parties in considering whether disputes are to be determined by arbitration or by legal proceedings, see the Standard Building Contract Guide. See also footnote [12].

■ Contract Particulars

1.1 Enter the length of the CDM Planning Period and the date it begins or ends. Compliance with the CDM Regulations means that sufficient time must be allocated for this task. It may be convenient for it to end on the Date of Possession or it may be necessary to allow time between the end of the Planning Period and the Date of Possession. Where Sections are used, it may be necessary to refer here to an additional sheet setting out the relevant dates for each Section. The sheet should be signed and dated by the parties and attached to the contract.

(SBC/AQ inserts an entry for 'Tender Price' being the total of the Contractor's prices)

1.1 Enter the date by which the Works should reach practical completion. Do not insert 'to be agreed', but you may insert a means by which the Date for Completion may be accurately calculated, e.g. 26 weeks from the 'Date of Possession'.

If Sections are to be used, delete the previous entry and insert the identifier of each Section and the relevant date. If there is insufficient space, refer to an additional sheet which should be signed and dated by the parties and attached to the contract.

1.7 Insert the relevant addresses of the parties for services of notices. Notices served to different addresses may not be valid.

2.4 Enter the date when the Contractor may take possession of the site. Unless Sections are used, the Contract assumes unimpeded possession of the whole site at this date.

If Sections are to be used, delete the previous entry and insert the identifier of each Section and the relevant date. If there is insufficient space, refer to an additional sheet which should be signed and dated by the parties and attached to the Contract.

Contract Particulars

1·1	CDM Planning Period [15]	shall mean the period of Six ~~* days~~/weeks * ending on the Date of Possession/ ~~* beginning/ending on~~ ~~_____ 20___~~
1·1	Date for Completion of the Works *(where completion by Sections does not apply)*	17 November 2012
	Sections: Dates for Completion of Sections [16]	~~Section ____ : _____~~ ~~Section ____ : _____~~ ~~Section ____ : _____~~
1·7	Addresses for service of notices by the Parties *(If none is stated, the address in each case, subject to clause 1·7·3, shall be that shown at the commencement of the Agreement.)* [17]	Employer As shown on page 1 of the Agreement Contractor As shown on page 1 of the Agreement
2·4	Date of Possession of the site *(where possession by Sections does not apply)*	12 December 20 11
	Sections: Dates of Possession of Sections [16]	~~Section ____ : _____ 20___~~ ~~Section ____ : _____ 20___~~ ~~Section ____ : _____ 20___~~

---

[15] Under the CDM Regulations 2007 every client is expressly required to allocate sufficient time (the CDM Planning Period) prior to the commencement of construction to enable contractors and others to carry out necessary CDM planning and preparation. There may be cases where that planning and preparation needs to be completed earlier than the Date of Possession and adaptation of the entries may be needed where there are Sections.

[16] Continue on further sheets if necessary, which should be signed or initialled by or on behalf of each Party and then be annexed to this Contract.

[17] As to service of notices etc. outside the United Kingdom, see the Standard Building Contract Guide.

Contract Particulars

2.5 Delete as appropriate to show if the deferment option applies. Enter period in weeks if less than six.

If Sections are to be used, delete the previous entry, delete as appropriate to show if the deferment option applies and, if so, insert the identifier of each Section and the relevant number of weeks if less than six. If there is insufficient space, refer to an additional sheet which should be signed and dated by the parties and attached to the Contract.

2.9.1.2 Delete to show whether the Contractor is required to show critical paths on its master programme. Normally, critical paths will be required.

2.19.3 If the Contractor's Designed Portion (CDP) is to be used, insert here the limit of the Contractor's liability for loss of use, etc. If no limit is intended, insert the words 'No Limit'.

2.32.2 Enter the rate of liquidated damages, which must be a genuine pre-estimate of the likely loss to the Employer resulting from the Contractor's failure to complete the Works by the Completion Date. State the period concerned, e.g. per day or per week. Inserting 'per week or part thereof' does not amount to allowing the damages to be calculated pro-rata and should be avoided. Do not enter 'Nil' or leave blank. If the Employer wishes to recover unliquidated damages at common law, an amendment of the contract with legal advice is required.

If Sections are to be used, delete the previous entry and insert the identifier of each Section and the relevant amount of liquidated damages. The rate of liquidated damages must be a genuine pre-estimate of the likely loss to the employer resulting from the Contractor's failure to complete each Section by its Completion Date. Take care that the amounts of damages are properly related to the anticipated loss if a particular Section is late and not simply the same sum for each Section (unless that is a true reflection of the anticipated loss in each case). If there is insufficient space, refer to an additional sheet which should be signed and dated by the parties and attached to the Contract. State the period concerned, e.g. per day or per week. Inserting 'per week or part thereof' does not amount to allowing the damages to be calculated pro-rata and should be avoided, because it may turn the damages into an unenforceable penalty. Do not enter 'Nil' or leave blank. If the Employer wishes to recover unliquidated damages at common law, an amendment of the Contract with legal advice is required.

2.37 Insert the relevant Section sums, the total of which will amount to the Contract Sum. If there is insufficient space, refer to an additional sheet which should be signed and dated by the parties and attached to the Contract.

2.38 Enter the Rectification Period. If nothing is entered, the period will be 6 months.

If Sections are to be used, delete the previous entry and insert the identifier of each Section and the relevant period. If nothing is entered, the period will be 6 months for each Section. If there is insufficient space, refer to an additional sheet which should be signed and dated by the parties and attached to the Contract.

2·5	Deferment of possession of the site *(where possession by Sections does not apply)*	Clause 2·5 * applies/~~does not apply~~ Maximum period of deferment (if less than 6 weeks) is Six weeks
	Sections: deferment of possession of Sections	~~Clause 2·5~~ * ~~applies/does not apply~~ ~~Maximum period of deferment (if less than 6 weeks) is[16]~~ ~~Section ____ : _____~~ ~~Section ____ : _____~~ ~~Section ____ : _____~~
2·9·1·2	Master programme	Critical paths * are/~~are not~~ required to be shown
2·19·3	Contractor's Designed Portion: limit of Contractor's liability for loss of use etc. (if any)	£ No limit
2·32·2	Liquidated damages *(where completion by Sections does not apply)*	at the rate of £ 950.00 per week
	Sections: rate of liquidated damages for each Section[16]	~~Section ____ : £ _____ per _____~~ ~~Section ____ : £ _____ per _____~~ ~~Section ____ : £ _____ per _____~~
2·37	Sections: Section Sums[16]	~~Section ____ : £ _____~~ ~~Section ____ : £ _____~~ ~~Section ____ : £ _____~~
2·38	Rectification Period *(where completion by Sections does not apply)* *(If no other period is stated, the period is 6 months.)*	Six months from the date of practical completion of the Works
	Sections: Rectification Periods[16] *(If no other period is stated, the period is 6 months.)*	~~Section ____ : _____ months~~ ~~Section ____ : _____ months~~ ~~Section ____ : _____ months~~ from the date of practical completion of each Section

Page 10 SBC/Q 2011 © The Joint Contracts Tribunal Limited 2011

Contract Particulars

4.8 This provision does not apply if the Employer is a local authority. Delete as appropriate to show whether advance payment applies. It is for the Employer to decide whether to make such a payment. Either an amount or a percentage of the Contract Sum may be inserted. Complete the details, showing the dates for repayment and amounts to be repaid on each date.

4.8 Delete as appropriate to show if a bond is required for the advance payment. If not deleted, a bond will be required.

4.9.1 Interim Certificates are to be issued regularly at monthly intervals until practical completion. Insert the due date of the first certificate. If no date is inserted, the first due date will be 1 month after the Date of Possession.

4.17.4 and 4.17.5

Materials, goods or items pre-fabricated for inclusion in the Works, but held off site, must be listed by the employer if their value is to be included in Interim Certificates. Clause 4.17.4 refers to uniquely identified items and clause 4.17.5 to not uniquely identified items. Consultation with the Employer must take place before the appropriate amounts of bonds are inserted. If a bond is not required for an entry, the entry should be deleted.

Contract Particulars

| 4·8 | Advance payment
(Not applicable where the Employer is a Local Authority) | Clause 4·8
* applies/~~does not apply~~

If applicable:
the advance payment will be[18]

£ 100,000.00 /

~~_____ per cent of the Contract Sum~~

and will be paid to the Contractor on

8 December 2011 ;

it will be reimbursed to the Employer in the following amount(s) and at the following time(s)

£10,000.00 in each certificate beginning with certificate No. 1 |

| 4·8 | Advance Payment Bond
(Not applicable where the Employer is a Local Authority)
(Where an advance payment is to be made, an advance payment bond is required unless stated that it is not required.) | An advance payment bond
* is/~~is not~~ required |

| 4·9·1 | Interim payments – due dates
(If no date is stated, the first due date is one month after the Date of Possession.) | The first due date is:

12 January 2012

and thereafter the same date in each month or the nearest Business Day in that month[19] |

| 4·17·4 | Listed Items – uniquely identified
(Delete the entry if no bond is required.) | * ~~For uniquely identified Listed Items a bond in respect of payment for such items is required for~~

£ _____ |

| 4·17·5 | Listed Items – not uniquely identified
(Delete the entry if clause 4·17·5 does not apply.) | * For Listed Items that are not uniquely identified a bond in respect of payment for such items is required for

£ _____ |

---

[18] Insert either a monetary amount or a percentage figure, delete the alternative and complete the other required details.

[19] The first date should not be more than one month after the Date of Possession. Where it is intended that interim payments should become due on the last day of each month, the entry may be completed/amended to read "the last day of *(insert month)* and thereafter the last day in each month or the nearest Business Day in that month." After practical completion, clause 4·9·1 allows for intervals of 2 months (or such other period as the Parties agree) between interim payments.

© The Joint Contracts Tribunal Limited 2011   SBC/Q 2011   Page 11

■ Contract Particulars

4.19 This provision does not apply if the Employer is a local authority. Delete as appropriate to show that a Retention Bond is required in lieu of a Retention percentage. An expiry date must also be inserted for the purpose of clause 6.3 of the bond. If no deletion is made and the particulars are not completed, the bond will not apply.

4.20.1 Insert the Retention percentage required. If nothing is inserted, the percentage will be 3%. To indicate that no Retention is required 'Nil' or '0' must be inserted.

4.21 and Schedule 7

Delete as appropriate to show which fluctuation Option is to apply. If no Option is selected, Option A will apply.

Options A or B

The fluctuation clauses (either Tax, etc. only under Option A or Full under Option B) provide for the addition of an amount to give the Contractor a truer reimbursement of increases paid. Enter a percentage figure if an additional sum is to be paid, otherwise enter 'Nil'.

Option C

The Formula Rules for the price adjustment formula require the Base Month to be entered (usually the calendar month prior to that in which the tender is to be returned). Delete as appropriate Parts I or II of section 2 of the Formula Rules. In the case of local authorities only, a percentage should be entered for the Non-Adjustable Element, or 'Nil' inserted. For a more detailed explanation see the Formula Rules, which are published separately.

(SBC/XQ inserts an entry for Daywork against clause 5.7)

6.4.1.2 Enter the minimum amount required for the Contractor's insurance against injury to persons or property. The amount entered does not affect the Contractor's liability, but it may limit the amount available to settle any claims. It is, therefore, important to insert a sum that is not too small.

Contract Particulars

4·19	Contractor's Retention Bond *(Not applicable where the Employer is a Local Authority)* *(Not applicable unless stated to apply and relevant particulars are given below)*	Clause 4·19 * ~~applies~~/does not apply ~~If clause 4·19 applies, the maximum aggregate sum for the purposes of clause 2 of the bond is~~ £ ~~_____~~ ~~For the purposes of clause 6·3 of the bond,~~ the expiry ~~date~~ shall be ~~_____~~
4·20·1	Retention Percentage *(The percentage is 3 per cent unless a different rate is stated; if no retention is required, insert 'Nil' or '0'.)*	Five _____ per cent
4·21 and Schedule 7	Fluctuations Options[20] *(If no Fluctuations Option is selected, Option A applies.)*	Schedule 7: * Fluctuations Option A applies/ * ~~Fluctuations Option B applies/~~ * ~~Fluctuations Option C applies~~
	Percentage addition for Fluctuations Option A, paragraph A·12 or Option B, paragraph B·13	Nil _____ per cent
	Formula Rules for Fluctuations Option C, paragraph C·1·2	~~Rule 3: Base Month~~ _____ 20____
	(For Local Authorities only)	Rule 3: Non-Adjustable Element _____ per cent
	(Unless Part II is stated to apply, Part I applies.)	Rules 10 and 30(i): * Part I/Part II of section 2 of the Formula ~~Rules applies[21]~~
6·4·1·2	Contractor's insurance: injury to persons or property – insurance cover *(for any one occurrence or series of occurrences arising out of one event)*	£ 2,000,000.00

---

[20] Delete all but one.

[21] The Part to be deleted depends upon which method of formula adjustment (Part I – Work Category Method or Part II – Work Group Method) is applicable.

■ Contract Particulars

6.5.1 Damage to property other than the Works can occur where there has been no negligence by the Contractor. If the Employer wishes to have insurance cover for such an occurrence, the appropriate deletion must be made and the minimum amount of insurance cover specified here. This is something which the employer should decide with the advice of an insurance advisor.

6.7 and Schedule 3

Delete as appropriate to show which of the clauses for insurance of the Works is to apply. Option A is for new buildings where the Contractor is to insure against All Risks. Option B is for new buildings where the Employer is to insure against All Risks. Option C is for existing structures and work in or extension to them where the Employer is to insure. The options should be explained to the Employer and the Employer's instructions obtained. If in doubt, the Employer should seek advice from an insurance expert.

6.7 and Schedule 3

The percentage fees of all professionals who may be involved in restoration must be entered.

If the Contractor is covered for the Works by an annual policy, the annual renewal date must be entered.

6.10 and Schedule 3

Details of the required terrorism cover must be inserted. Where the information is in a document, refer to the document which should be signed and dated by the parties and attached to the contract. If nothing is inserted, Pool Re Cover will be required.

6.12 If the Contractor's Designed Portion (CDP) is to be used, delete as appropriate to indicate the level of professional indemnity insurance cover required. If no deletion is made, the level will be the aggregate amount for any one period of insurance (the period is a year). The amount should be entered. If no amount is entered, no insurance is required.

The level of cover for pollution/contamination claims should be entered. If no amount is entered, no cover is required. This is something which the Employer should decide with the advice of an insurance advisor.

Delete as appropriate to indicate the required period of insurance – either 6 or 12 years. If no deletion is made, the period will be 6 years. If the Contract is executed as a deed, thereby providing a 12-year limitation period, it makes sense to delete the 6 years option so as to require insurance for the full 12 years also. Although it is possible to require the insurance for a period in excess of 12 years, it would be highly unusual.

Contract Particulars

6·5·1	Insurance – liability of Employer *(Not required unless it is stated that it may be required and the minimum amount of indemnity is stated)*	Insurance * ~~may be required~~/is not required ~~Minimum amount of indemnity for any one occurrence~~ or series of occurrences arising out of one event £ _____ [22]
6·7 and Schedule 3	Insurance of the Works – Insurance Options[20][23]	Schedule 3: * Insurance Option A applies/ * ~~Insurance Option B applies/~~ * ~~Insurance Option C applies~~
6·7 and Schedule 3 Insurance Option A (paragraphs A·1 and A·3), B (paragraph B·1) or C (paragraph C·2)	Percentage to cover professional fees *(If no other percentage is stated, it shall be 15 per cent.)*	Nine _____ per cent
6·7 and Schedule 3 Insurance Option A (paragraph A·3)	Annual renewal date of insurance *(as supplied by the Contractor)*	1 April
6·10 and Schedule 3	Terrorism Cover – details of the required cover *(State reference numbers and dates or other identifiers of documents setting out the requirements. Unless otherwise stated, Pool Re Cover is required.)*	Document TC/350
6·12	Contractor's Designed Portion (CDP) Professional Indemnity insurance	
	Level of cover *(If an alternative is not selected the amount shall be the aggregate amount for any one period of insurance. A period of insurance for these purposes shall be one year unless otherwise stated.)*	Amount of indemnity required * relates to claims or series of claims arising out of one event/ * ~~is the aggregate amount for any one period of insurance~~
	(If no amount is stated, insurance under clause 6·12 shall not be required.)	and is £ 500,000.00
	Cover for pollution and contamination claims *(If no amount is stated, such cover shall not be required; unless otherwise stated, the required limit of indemnity is an annual aggregate amount.)*	* ~~is required, with a sub-limit of indemnity of~~ £ _____ / * is not required

---

[22] If the indemnity is to be for an aggregate amount and not for any one occurrence or series of occurrences the entry should be amended to make this clear.

[23] Obtaining Terrorism Cover, which is necessary in order to comply with the requirements of Insurance Option A, B or C, will involve an additional premium and may in certain situations be difficult to effect. Where a difficulty arises discussion should take place between the Parties and their insurance advisers. See the Standard Building Contract Guide.

Contract Particulars

6.14 Delete as appropriate to show whether the Joint Fire Code is to apply. If so, state whether the insurers of the Works rate the Works as a 'Large Project'.

6.17 Delete as appropriate depending upon whether the Employer or the Contractor is to bear the cost of complying with revisions to the Joint Fire Code made after the Base Date.

7.2 Assignment of the right to bring an action against the Contractor by a future purchaser or tenant could be a requirement of the Employer. Instructions must be taken before tenders are invited. If no deletions are made, the provision will apply.

If Sections are to be used and the rights are not to apply to all Sections, delete the previous entry and insert the identifier of each Section and the relevant details. Otherwise, delete this entry. If there is insufficient space, refer to an additional sheet which should be signed and dated by the parties and attached to the contract.

8.9.2 Enter periods of suspension. If nothing is entered, the period will be 2 months.

8.11.1.1 to 8.11.1.5

Enter periods of suspension. If nothing is entered, the period will be 2 months.

9.2.1 If the parties wish to name an Adjudicator to which disputes will be referred, the name should be entered here. Whether or not an Adjudicator is entered, delete as appropriate to indicate the chosen nominator. It should be noted that, if there is no named Adjudicator and no chosen nominator, the referring party may apply to any of the listed nominators.

9.4.1 Delete as appropriate to indicate which body will appoint the Arbitrator. If no deletions are made, the appointer will be the President or a Vice-President of the Royal Institute of British Architects.

Contract Particulars

	Expiry of required period of CDP Professional Indemnity insurance is *(If no period is selected, the expiry date shall be 6 years from the date of practical completion of the Works.)*	* ~~6 years/~~ * 12 years/ * _____ years (not exceeding 12 years)	
6·14	Joint Fire Code	The Joint Fire Code * applies/~~does not apply~~[24]	
	If the Joint Fire Code applies, state whether the insurer under Schedule 3, Insurance Option A, B or C (paragraph C·2) has specified that the Works are a 'Large Project':	* ~~Yes~~/No[24]	
6·17	Joint Fire Code – amendments/revisions *(The cost shall be borne by the Contractor unless otherwise stated.)*	The cost, if any, of compliance with amendment(s) or revision(s) to the Joint Fire Code shall be borne by * ~~the Employer~~/the Contractor	
7·2	Assignment/grant by Employer of rights under clause 7·2 *(If neither entry is deleted, clause 7·2 applies.)*	Clause 7·2 * ~~applies~~/does not apply	
	Sections: rights under clause 7·2 *(If clause 7·2 applies, amend the entry if rights under that clause are to apply to certain Sections only.)*	* ~~Rights under clause 7·2 apply to each Section~~	
8·9·2	Period of suspension *(If none is stated, the period is 2 months.)*	2 months	
8·11·1·1 to 8·11·1·5	Period of suspension *(If none is stated, the period is 2 months.)*	2 months	
9·2·1	Adjudication[25]	The Adjudicator is I M Wright	
	Nominating body – where no Adjudicator is named or where the named Adjudicator is unwilling or unable to act (whenever that is established)[26] *(Where an Adjudicator is not named and a nominating body has not been selected, the nominating body shall be one of the bodies listed opposite selected by the Party requiring the reference to adjudication.)*	* Royal Institute of British Architects * ~~The Royal Institution of Chartered Surveyors~~ * ~~constructionadjudicators.com~~[27] * ~~Association of Independent Construction Adjudicators~~[28] * ~~Chartered Institute of Arbitrators~~	

---

[24] Where Insurance Option A applies these entries are made on information supplied by the Contractor.

[25] The Parties should either name the Adjudicator and select the nominating body or, alternatively, select only the nominating body. The Adjudication Agreement (Adj) and the Adjudication Agreement (Named Adjudicator) (Adj/N) have been prepared by JCT for use when appointing an Adjudicator.

[26] Delete all but one of the nominating bodies asterisked.

[27] constructionadjudicators.com is a trading name of Contractors Legal Grp Ltd.

[28] Association of Independent Construction Adjudicators acts as an agent of and is controlled by the National Specialist Contractors' Council for the purpose of the nomination of adjudicators.

■ Contract Particulars

Part 2: Third Party Rights and Collateral Warranties

The Particulars must be completed if third party rights or warranties from the contractor, or warranties from the sub-contractors, are required.

(A) This should be completed with the names, class or description of the purchasers and/or tenants who are to be given rights. This must be as precise as possible (e.g. 'Clothewell Tailoring' or 'all first purchasers'). Rights can only be conferred on the parties identified. The part of the Works to be let must also be identified, and it is important in each case to state whether rights are to be conferred as third party rights (clause 7A) or whether as a collateral warranty (clause 7C). If no clause is specified, clause 7A will apply.

(B) Whether rights are to be conferred as third party rights or by collateral warranty, this section is to be completed. The clause numbers refer to either the warranty CWa/P&T or Part 1 of Schedule 5.

    1.1.2   Delete as applicable whether or not the Contractor is to be additionally liable for any other losses incurred by the purchaser or tenant. If paragraph 1.1.2 applies, insert the amount of maximum liability desired.

             If no deletion is made and the maximum liability is not stated, clause 1.1.2 will not apply.

             Delete as appropriate to indicate whether the type of maximum liability is to be for each breach or as an aggregate limit. If no deletion is made, the type of liability limit will be aggregate.

    1.3.1   For the purposes of the net contribution clause, the consultants must be listed. If none are listed, they will be the Architect or Contract Administrator, the Quantity Surveyor and any other consultants who agree to give warranties or the equivalent to purchasers and/or tenants.

    1.3.2   For the purposes of the net contribution clause, the sub-contractors must be listed. If none are listed, they will be those who agree to give warranties or the equivalent to purchasers and/or tenants.

(C) This should be completed with the names, class or description of the funder who is to be given rights. If no entry is made, funder rights are not required from the Contractor.

(D) Whether rights are to be conferred as third party rights or by collateral warranty, this section is to be completed. The clause numbers refer to either the warranty CWa/F or Part 2 of Schedule 5.

    Third party rights or collateral warranty must be chosen. If not, third party rights applies.

    1.1   Unless this is completed differently, the consultants and sub-contractors will be those listed (or deemed to be listed) under (B).

(E) If collateral warranties are required from sub-contractors, the details may be inserted in this section.

    3.7 and 3.9

        The sub-contractors must be identified or, if not then known, the category must be stated (e.g. 'electrical'). In each instance, state the type of warranty required:

        SCWa/P&T – Purchaser/tenant

        SCWa/F – Funder

        SCWa/E – Employer.

Where a sub-contractor has any design responsibility, the level of professional indemnity insurance must also be stated.

Attestation

There are two options. The first is to execute the Contract under hand (a simple contract). The other option is to execute the Contract as a deed (a specialty contract). There are several differences. One is that contracts executed as deeds do not require consideration in order to make them legally binding on the parties. Another and, in the context of this Contract, more important difference is that there is a 6-year limitation period for contracts under hand and a 12-year limitation period for contracts executed as deeds. The significance of that must be explained to the Employer before tenders are invited, and the Employer's instructions must be obtained. If it is decided to execute the Contract as a deed, it should be noted that this can be done by sealing or by signing. The notes in the Contract clearly explain how each of the options is to be completed. Three methods of execution of a deed by a company are shown.

The contract administration forms

Clerk of Works Direction (published by the Institute of Clerks of Works by agreement with the RIBA)

Architect's/Contract Administrator's Instruction

Interim Certificate

Statement of Retention

Statement of Reimbursement

Notice of Partial Possession by the Employer

Notification of Extension of Time

Non-Completion Certificate

Practical Completion Certificate

Section Completion Certificate

Certificate of Making Good

Final Certificate

Clerk of Works Direction

Clause 3.4

Use

Directions may be given to the Contractor by the Clerk of Works in respect of matters about which the Architect is empowered to issue instructions under the Contract.

The Contractor must not act solely on the basis of a direction, and it will be of no contractual effect unless confirmed by an Architect's Instruction (AI) within 2 working days. Nevertheless, it can still be a useful early-warning device. If greater powers are to be given to the Clerk of Works, as is the case with some local authorities, these must be clearly set out in the Contract, not simply included as a clause in the Preliminaries to the Contract Bills or specification.

Be careful before confirming a Clerk of Works Direction in case there are CDM Regulations implications which should first be referred to the CDM Co-ordinator for comment.

Completing

The form is published by the Institute of Clerks of Works by agreement with the RIBA. The name and address of the Architect, Employer and Contractor should correspond with the entries in the Articles of Agreement of the contract. The location of the Works (an abbreviated entry) and Contract Date provide precise information and should correspond with entries in the Articles and Recitals of the contract. The job reference will be the Architect's office reference for the project, and the direction number should be inserted. The issue date is important, given that the Architect's confirmation is required within 2 working days.

The matter of financial and other implications should be dealt with in the Architect's Instructions.

Issue

The Clerk of Works should send the original to the Contractor, and a duplicate to the Architect at the same time. In practice, a copy will usually be given to the Contractor's person-in-charge and a copy sent immediately to the Architect, perhaps after a telephone call alerting the Architect as to its content. An exact copy should be placed in the site records file.

Clerk of Works Direction

Architect/CA: Ivor Barch Associates
address: Prospects Drive, Fairbridge

Employer: Cosmeston Prep School
address: Fairbridge

Contractor: L&M Construction Ltd
address: Ferry Road, Fairbridge

Works situated at: New School Library
Park Street, Fairbridge

Contract dated: 7 December 2011

Job reference: IBA/05/20

Direction no: 6

Issue date: 16 February 2012

Under the terms of the above-mentioned Contract, I issue the following direction.

This direction shall be of no effect unless confirmed in writing by the Architect/Contract Administrator within 2 working days, and does not authorise any extra payment.

Direction

1. MORTAR MIXES
   The mortar mixes are as follows:

   Blockwork below dpc 1:3
   Blockwork above dpc 1:1:6
   Brickwork below dpc (below ground level) 1:3
   Brickwork below dpc (above ground level) 1:3
   (pointing in 2:1:8)
   Brickwork above dpc 2:1:9
   Coloured mortar is to be Zilcon mortar, ref. Y73.

2. REDUCED LEVELS
   Excavate to revised levels to remove unsuitable material where indicated on site.

Signed *John Fox-Talbot* Clerk of Works

Covered by Instruction no:

Distribution: ☐ Contractor ☐ Architect/CA ☐ ☐ Site records file

SBC

Architect's/Contract Administrator's Instruction

Clause 3.10

Use

Instructions should be in writing or, if oral, confirmed in writing. Use the forms in preference to writing a letter, as it is then clearly perceived as an instruction and is recorded as such.

Empowered necessary instructions (SHALL) might refer to:

- discrepancies and divergences (2.15, 2.16.1, 2.17.2);
- issue of further drawings or details (2.11, 2.12);
- levels and setting out (2.10);
- defects arising in the Rectification Period (2.38);
- expenditure of Provisional Sums (3.16);
- discovery of antiquities (3.22.2).

Empowered discretionary instructions (MAY) refer to:

- instructions for integration of CDP work (2.2.2);
- errors in setting out not to be amended (2.10);
- defects to be rectified during Rectification Period (2.38);
- defects in Rectification Period not to be amended (2.38);
- confirmation of Clerk of Works Directions (3.4);
- variations (3.14);
- postponement (3.15);
- testing, opening up (3.17);
- work not in accordance with the contract (3.18);
- work not carried out in a proper and workmanlike manner (3.19);
- exclusion of persons (3.21);
- insurance matters, where applicable (6.5).

An Architect's Instruction which might have health and safety implications should first be sent in draft to the CDM Co-ordinator for comment. Depending on the content, the Contractor might need to adjust the Construction Phase Plan, compliance with which is a contractual obligation.

Completing

The name and address of issuer, Employer and Contractor should correspond with entries in the Articles of Agreement of the Contract. The signature on the form should be that of, or on behalf of, the issuer named in Article 3. The location of the Works (an abbreviated entry) and Contract Date provide precise information and should correspond with entries in the Articles and Recitals of the Contract. The job reference will be the office reference for the project, and the instruction number should be inserted.

It is advisable to state the Contract clause number which empowers each instruction.

If this is not done, the Contractor, under clause 3.13, may request confirmation of the empowering clause.

Where an instruction has known or agreed financial implications, these should be entered. Where there is no financial implication, strike a line through the columns. Where it is intended that work will be at no extra cost to the Employer, this should be made absolutely clear.

The contract administration forms

Architect's/Contract Administrator's Instruction

Architect's Instruction

Issued by: Ivor Barch Associates
address: Prospects Drive, Fairbridge

Employer: Cosmeston Prep School
address: Fairbridge

Contractor: L&M Construction Ltd
address: Ferry Road, Fairbridge

Works: New School Library
situated at: Park Street, Fairbridge

Contract dated: 7 December 2011

Job reference: IBA/05/20

Instruction no: 4

Issue date: 17 February 2012

Sheet: 1 of 2

Under the terms of the above-mentioned Contract, I/we issue the following instructions:

Instruction	Office use: Approximate costs £ omit	£ add
1. INCOMING GAS MAIN Accepted the quotation ref. no. 8438/63 dated 6 January 2012 received from EuroGas in the sum of £248.00 for the new incoming gas main and supply and installation of gas meter. A copy of their quotation is attached. This sum is to be set against the provisional sum of £400 included under ref. 3/2G in the bill of quantities.	400.00	248.00
2. (a) HIP TILES OMIT: Farland concrete third round hip tiles, bill of quantities ref. 5/15E. ADD in lieu: Red bank 300mm long red Terracotta third round segmental ridge tiles, list no. 259.	372.00	514.00
(b) HIP IRONS OMIT: 4 no. hip irons, bill of quantities ref no. 5/15F. ADD in lieu 4 no. Red Bank 300mm long red Terracotta Scroll hip finial tiles 225mm diameter. Hip tiles and finial tiles to be obtained from Fairbridge Bank Manufacturing Co. Ltd.	–	–
3. PICTURE-HANGING FACILITIES IN ACTIVITIES ROOM Supply and fix aluminium picture rail approx. 12m long and 100 no. type (b) U-shaped hooks obtainable from Library Aids of Fairbridge. Picture rail to be fixed in location shown on attached drawing no. IBA/94/20/61 at 2050mm from finished floor level.	–	80.00
(continued)		
Signed *Ivor Barch*	772.00	842.00

To be signed by or for the issuer named above

Amount of Contract Sum £
± Approximate value of previous Instructions £
Sub-total £
± Approximate value of this Instruction £
Approximate adjusted total £

Distribution:
☐ Contractor ☐ Structural Engineer ☐ CDM Co-ordinator ☐
☐ Employer ☐ M&E Consultant ☐
☐ Quantity Surveyor ☐ Clerk of Works ☐ File

for SBC / IC / ICD / MW / MWD   CONTRACT ADMINISTRATION FORMS   © RIBA Publishing 2011

■ Architect's/Contract Administrator's Instruction

The Contractor's attention should be drawn to particular items in the Architect's Instruction which are likely to have health and safety implications. A footnote might be added to the AI such as 'Any adjustments thought necessary to your Construction Phase Plan should be submitted to us and direct to the Employer and the CDM Co-ordinator for information'.

Issue

Send the original to the Contractor and a duplicate to the Employer at the same time. Send copies to the Quantity Surveyor, CDM Co-ordinator if appointed, other consultants and Clerk of Works, as applicable. File an exact copy.

A printed continuation sheet is available.

Where the Contract Administrator is not an Architect, a Contract Administrator's Instruction should be used.

Clerk of Work's Directions must be confirmed within 2 days (clause 3.4).

Instructions issued otherwise than in writing must be confirmed within 7 days by the Contractor unless already confirmed by the Architect. The Architect has 7 days from receiving the Contractor's confirmation in which to dissent in writing. If the Contractor has complied with instructions which have not been confirmed by either Architect or Contractor, the Architect may confirm such instructions in writing at any time up to the issue of the Final Certificate (clause 3.12).

Architect's/Contract Administrator's Instruction

Instruction *continuation*

Issued by: Ivor Barch Associates
address: Prospects Drive, Fairbridge

Job reference: IBA/05/20

Instruction no: 4

Issue date: 17 February 2012

Sheet: 2 of 2

	£ omit	£ add
Brought forward:	772.00	842.00
4. VELUX ROOFLIGHTS OMIT: double glazing with 4mm thick coated float glass outer sheet, bill of quantities ref. 5/25B. ADD in lieu: double glazing 2x3mm laminated float glass outer sheet.	–	–
5. MORTAR MIXES This is to confirm Clerk of Works Direction no 6. that mortar mixes are as follows: Blockwork below dpc 1:3 Blockwork above dpc 1:1:6 Brickwork below dpc (below ground level) 1:3 Brickwork below dpc (above ground level) 1:3 (pointing in 2:1:8) Brickwork below dpc (above ground) 1.3 (pointing in 2:1:8) Coloured mortar is to be Zilcon mortar, ref. Y73.	–	–
6. REDUCED LEVELS This is to confirm Clerk of Works Direction no. 6. Excavate to revised levels to remove unsuitable material. The 'as dug' levels as shown on the record made by the site foreman and clerk of works are agreed.	–	–
This instruction is issued in accordance with clauses 3.14 and 3.16 of the contract. (Item nos. 4, 5 and 6 are to be at no cost to the Employer.)		

To be signed by or for the issuer named above

Signed *Ivor Barch*

	£ omit	£ add
	772.00	842.00

Amount of Contract Sum	£ 505,096.00
± Approximate value of previous Instructions	£ 500.00
Sub-total	£ 505,596.00
± Approximate value of this Instruction	£ 70.00
Approximate adjusted total	£ 505,666.00

■ Architect's/Contract Administrator's Instruction

Contract Administrator's Instruction

Issued by:
address:

Employer:
address:

Contractor:
address:

Works:
situated at:

Contract dated:

Job reference:

Instruction no:

Issue date:

Sheet: of

Under the terms of the above-mentioned Contract, I/we issue the following instructions:

	Office use: Approximate costs	
	£ omit	£ add

To be signed by or for the issuer named above

Signed _____

Amount of Contract Sum £
± Approximate value of previous Instructions £
Sub-total £
± Approximate value of this Instruction £
Approximate adjusted total £

Distribution
☐ Contractor   ☐ Structural Engineer   ☐ CDM Co-ordinator   ☐
☐ Employer   ☐ M&E Consultant   ☐
☐ Quantity Surveyor ☐ Clerk of Works   ☐ File

for SBC / IC / ICD / MW / MWD   CONTRACT ADMINISTRATION FORMS   © RIBA Publishing 2011

Interim Certificate

Clauses 4.9 to 4.13

Use

The amendments to the Housing Grants, Construction and Regeneration Act 1996 which have been effected as a result of the Local Democracy, Economic Development and Construction Act 2009 have been reflected in changes to the certification and payment provisions of the Contract. The Architect must still certify the amount of interim payment to be made by the Employer to the Contractor, but other things have changed including the provisions for notices.

Clause 4.9.1 states that the due dates for interim payments are as set out in the Contract Particulars, monthly until practical completion and thereafter two monthly until the expiry of the Rectification Period or the issue of the Certificate of Making Good, whichever is the later. Clause 4.10.1 requires the Architect to issue each Interim Certificate no later than 5 days after each due date. The certificate must state the amount due at the due date to the Contractor, calculated in accordance with clause 4.9.2. It must specify also to what the amount relates and the basis on which the amount was calculated. This requirement might be met by attaching a copy, or a brief summary, of the valuation by the Quantity Surveyor. Alternatively, a specially prepared statement might be appended.

The Contractor may make an Interim Application to the Quantity Surveyor no later than 7 days before the due date, stating the sum the Contractor considers will become due on the due date and showing the basis on which it has been calculated.

If the Architect fails to issue an Interim Certificate in accordance with clause 4.10.1 and the Contractor has made an Interim Application, that application becomes an Interim Payment Notice. A Contractor which has not made an Interim Application may give an Interim Payment Notice to the Quantity Surveyor at any time after the 5-day period noted in clause 4.10.1, stating the sum the Contractor considers became due on the due date and showing the basis on which it has been calculated. It is obviously important that the Architect issues the Interim Certificate on time.

The final date for payment of an interim payment is 14 days after its due date. The sum to be paid by the Employer is the sum stated in the Interim Certificate. If there is no Interim Certificate, the sum to be paid is the sum stated in the Interim Payment Notice. If the Interim Payment Notice has been given by the Contractor following the Architect's failure to issue an Interim Certificate in time, the final date for payment is postponed by the number of days after the expiry of the 5-day period in clause 4.10.1 that the Interim Payment Notice was given.

An Employer who wishes to pay less than the amount stated as due in the Interim Certificate or in the Interim Payment Notice, must give a Pay Less Notice to the Contractor no later than 5 days before the final date for payment.

The Pay Less Notice must state the amount the Employer considers is due and the basis of calculation. It should be noted that a Pay Less Notice may be given on the Employer's behalf by the Architect, Quantity Surveyor or any other person notified to the Contractor as authorised by the Employer to do so. It may not be given until an Interim Certificate or an Interim Payment Notice has been issued. Note that under clause 4.12.6 interest will become payable if the Employer fails to pay sums properly due within the prescribed period.

Interim Certificate

Issued by: Ivor Barch Associates
address: Prospects Drive, Fairbridge

Employer: Cosmeston Prep School
address: Fairbridge

Contractor: L&M Construction Ltd
address: Ferry Road, Fairbridge

Works situated at: New School Library
Park Street, Fairbridge

Contract dated: 7 December 2011

Job reference: IBA/05/20
Certificate no: 8
Date of valuation: 9 August 2012
Due date: 13 August 2012
Date of issue: 15 August 2012
Final date for payment: 27 August 2012

This Interim Certificate is issued under the terms of the above-mentioned Contract.

Gross Valuation (calculation attached)	£ 347,260.00
Less Retention as detailed on the attached Statement of Retention	£ 17,363.00
Sub-total	£ 329,897.00
Less reimbursement of advance payment (statement attached)	£ 80,000.00
Sub-total	£ 249.897.00
Less total amount previously certified	£ 208,133.00
Sub-total	£ 41,764.00
Less payments referred to in clause 4.9.2.4	£ —
Net amount for payment	£ 41,764.00

All amounts are exclusive of VAT. The Employer shall in addition pay the amount of VAT properly chargeable.

I/We hereby certify that the **amount due** to the Contractor from the Employer is (in words)

Forty One Thousand Seven Hundred and Sixty Four pounds only

Signed *Ivor Barch*

To be signed by or for the issuer named above

This is not a Tax Invoice.

Distribution: ☐ Employer ☐ Contractor ☐ Quantity Surveyor ☐ File copy

for SBC   CONTRACT ADMINISTRATION FORMS   © RIBA Publishing 2011

Interim Certificate

Completing

Enter the name and address of issuer, Employer and Contractor. Enter the location of the Works (abbreviated) and the Contract Date to give precise identification. Enter the office job reference, and a sequential number of the certificate relating to that Contract. Enter the date of valuation, the due date, the date of issue of the certificate and the final date for payment which will be 14 days added to the due date. Therefore, if the due date is the 12th, the final date for payment will be the 26th (see clause 4.12.1). These rules are very important in relation to the Contract conditions.

Enter details of payment certified:

Gross valuation – calculated in accordance with clause 4.16 and includes, for example:

- total value of work properly executed by the Contractor;
- total value of unfixed materials and goods properly on site;
- value of 'listed items' off site stated as being due.

Less amounts deductible – includes, for example:

- amounts which may be retained by the Employer as detailed on the Statement of Retention, which should be attached to the certificate;
- amount of any advance payment due for reimbursement as detailed in the Statement of Reimbursement which should be attached to the certificate.

Less the total amount previously certified

- (note that this refers to 'certified', not necessarily 'paid').

Less any amounts referred to in clause 4.9.2.4

Enter the resulting net amount certified for payment under this certificate. Entry is to be in figures, followed by words. (All these figures are exclusive of VAT.)

The signature on the certificate should be that of, or on behalf of, the issuer named in Article 3.

Note that the amounts certified are exclusive of VAT. It is for the Contractor to recover VAT by means of a VAT invoice after receipt of the Interim Certificate from the Architect.

Issue

Send the certificate to the Employer and to the Contractor at the same time. Remember to attach a statement showing what the amount relates to and how calculated, and the Statement of Retention and where appropriate a Statement of Reimbursement of advance payment. Send a copy of each to the Quantity Surveyor.

Although, under clause 4.10.2, it is for the Architect to decide if valuations are necessary, in practice it will be rare for the Architect to issue a certificate without first getting the Quantity Surveyor's valuation. The valuation should be made no earlier than 7 days before the date of issue of the Interim Certificate to which it relates (clause 4.16).

Statement of Retention

Clause 4.18.2

Use

At the date of each Interim Certificate, the Architect must prepare a statement showing the Retention deducted from the Contractor and, where relevant, the amount to be released. This is usually set out in a Statement of Retention prepared by the Quantity Surveyor and submitted with the valuation. Copies can be made of this and attached to the Interim Certificate.

Completing

The name and address of the issuer should correspond with the entry in Article 3 of the Contract. The location of the Works (an abbreviated entry) should correspond with the entry in the Recitals of the Contract. The job reference will be the office reference for the project. The number of the certificate to which the statement relates provides precise identification. The issue date should be that of the certificate.

Enter the gross valuation of the amount due to the Contractor and the applicable Retention. Where Sections are involved, or if the Employer has taken part of the Works or any Section into partial possession, it is likely that there may be two or even three categories of Retention applicable to varying amounts.

Issue

Send the original to the Employer, attached to the certificate to which the statement relates. Attach a duplicate to the certificate sent to the Contractor at the same time. Send a copy to the Quantity Surveyor. File an exact and fully completed copy.

Statement of Retention

Issued by: Ivor Barch Associates
address: Prospects Drive, Fairbridge

Works: New School Library
situated at: Park Street, Fairbridge

Job reference: IBA/05/20
Relating to Certificate No: 8
Issue Date: 15 August 2012

	Gross valuation (£)	Amount of retention (£)
Amount subject to **Full** retention of 5 %	£347,260.00	£17,363.00
Amount subject to **Half** retention of 2½ %		
Amount subject to **Nil** retention of ___ %		
Total	£347,260.00	£17,363.00

All amounts are exclusive of VAT.

for SBC   CONTRACT ADMINISTRATION FORMS   © RIBA Publishing 2011

Statement of Reimbursement

Clause 4.8

Use

If the Employer has decided to make an advance payment to the Contractor, the Contractor must have first provided a bond such as the one included in the Contract. The Contract Particulars state the way in which the Contractor is to reimburse the Employer. Usually the amount will be reimbursed in stages for the duration of the project (say monthly), deducted from the gross valuation each month and noted on the Interim Certificate. The Contract does not require a Statement of Reimbursement, but it is a useful record of the stages of reimbursement of what in some cases may be a substantial sum of money.

Completing

The name and address of the issuer should correspond with the entry in Article 3 of the Contract. The location of the Works (an abbreviated entry) should correspond with the entry in the Recitals of the Contract. The job reference will be the office reference for the project. The number of the certificate to which the statement relates provides precise identification. The issue date should be that of the certificate.

Enter the amount of the payment advanced by the Employer, the total of the previous reimbursements, the reimbursement relevant to the Interim Certificate to which the statement relates and the cumulative reimbursement (i.e. the total of the previous reimbursements plus the current reimbursement).

Issue

Send the original to the Employer, attached to the certificate to which the statement relates. Attach a duplicate to the certificate sent to the Contractor at the same time. Send a copy to the Quantity Surveyor. File an exact and fully completed copy.

Statement of Reimbursement
of advance payment

Issued by: Ivor Barch Associates
address: Prospects Drive, Fairbridge

Works: New School Library
situated at: Park Street, Fairbridge

Job reference: IBA/05/20

Relating to Certificate no: 8

Issue date: 15 August 2012

	Amount of advance payment	Total previous reimbursement	Reimbursement on this Application	Cumulative reimbursement*
	£	£	£	£
Main Contractor	100,000.00	70,000.00	10,000.00	80,000.00
Total	100,000.00	70,000.00	10,000.00	80,000.00

* It is the total cumulative reimbursement that should be entered on the payment certificate.

SBC / IC / ICD CONTRACT ADMINISTRATION FORMS © RIBA Publishing 2011

Notice of Partial Possession by the Employer

Clauses 2.33 to 2.37

Use

If clause 2.33 is implemented, then in the event of partial possession the Architect must issue a written notice identifying the date on which partial possession took place, referred to as the 'Relevant Date', and identifying the 'Relevant Part' of the Works taken over by the Employer. Possession is subject to the Contractor's consent, which must not be unreasonably withheld or delayed, and the notice is issued on behalf of the Employer.

Where the Works are divided into Sections, it is conceivable that the Employer may take partial possession of several parts of several Sections.

Practical completion is deemed to have occurred for certain purposes, and the Rectification Period is deemed to have commenced on the Relevant Date.

Care should be taken to keep the CDM Co-ordinator informed because for certain purposes practical completion is deemed to have occurred and the construction phase for the relevant part may be over. There could be implications concerning the Contractor's obligations under clause 3.23.4 and information for the health and safety file.

Completing

The name and address of issuer, Employer and Contractor should correspond with entries in the Articles of Agreement of the Contract. The signature on the notice should be that of, or on behalf of, the issuer named in Article 3. The location of the Works (an abbreviated entry) and Contract Date provide precise identification, and should correspond with entries in the Articles and Recitals of the Contract. The job reference will be the office reference for the project, and the notice number will be sequential for the particular project.

Enter details of the partial possession as precisely as possible. When identifying the relevant part, show its extent – and it is useful to refer to an annexed drawing. Define the boundaries beyond all doubt. Pay particular attention to the boundaries between floors, and include cross-sectional drawings to make the line of separation absolutely clear. Enter the relevant date, and if appropriate give a precise time as well.

The implications of partial possession are clearly set out in clauses 2.34 to 2.37 inclusive.

Issue

Send the original to the Contractor and a duplicate to the Employer at the same time. Send copies to the Quantity Surveyor, CDM Co-ordinator if appointed, other consultants and Clerk of Works, as applicable. File an exact copy.

Note: It is sound practice to note on the file copy of the statement the date the Rectification Period ends.

Partial possession should not be confused with the contract provision found in clause 2.6 which allows for storage, use or occupation by the employer while the Works are still in the possession of the contractor. Partial possession should not be confused with, or used instead of, Section Completion, which anticipates phasing from the outset.

Notice of Partial Possession by the Employer

Issued by: Ivor Barch Associates
address: Prospects Drive, Fairbridge

Employer: Cosmeston Prep School
address: Fairbridge

Contractor: L&M Construction Ltd
address: Ferry Road, Fairbridge

Works situated at: New School Library, Park Street, Fairbridge

Contract dated: 7 December 2011

Job reference: IBA/05/20
Statement no: 1
Issue date: 23 November 2012

Under the terms of the above-mentioned Contract,

I/we hereby give notice that a part of the Works, namely

The Library Activities Room, stores and offices adjacent, all as outlined in red on the attached drawing no. IBA/94/20/87

was taken into possession by the Employer on

23 November 20 12

To be signed by or for the issuer named above on behalf of the Employer

Signed *Ivor Barch*

Distribution: Contractor, Employer, Nominated Sub-Contractors, Quantity Surveyor, Structural Engineer, M&E Consultant, Clerk of Works, CDM Co-ordinator, File

for SBC / IC / ICD — CONTRACT ADMINISTRATION FORMS — © RIBA Publishing 2011

Notification of Extension of Time

Clause 2.28

Use

If the Contractor gives written notice of delay, and if in the opinion of the Architect the cause of delay is an event which is likely to delay completion of the Works beyond the Completion Date, then the Architect is obliged to make in writing a fair and reasonable extension of time.

The notification should state which Relevant Events have been taken into account, the allocation of extension of time to each and the reduction in time attributed to each Relevant Omission. Note that the Architect is required to respond to every valid notice, even if of the opinion that no extension of time is to be given. If reasonably practicable, notification should be made within 12 weeks from the receipt of the required particulars from the Contractor. The Architect must endeavour to notify the Contractor before the Completion Date if it occurs before the expiry of the 12 weeks. It should be noted that failure of the Architect to give notice of an extension of time within these timescales will not deprive the Contractor of the right to an extension and the Architect has the opportunity to review the situation during the 12 weeks following practical completion of the Works or any Section.

The notification form may be used for delays during the progress of the Works, in a situation where the Contractor has already overrun the Completion Date but not yet reached practical completion, or for the mandatory review period of up to 12 weeks after practical completion as set out in clause 2.28.5.

Where the Works have been divided into Sections, the reference to the Works in the notification must be deleted, because references to the Completion Date will then apply to the numbered Section only.

Completing

The name and address of issuer, Employer and Contractor should correspond with entries in the Articles of Agreement of the Contract. The signature on the form should be that of, or on behalf of, the issuer named in Article 3. The location of the Works (an abbreviated entry) and Contract Date provide precise identification, and should correspond with entries in the Articles and Recitals of the Contract. The job reference will be the office reference for the project, and the notification number should be inserted.

The Completion Dates, both as previously fixed and revised, must be entered, and it is necessary to state which Relevant Events and/or Relevant Omissions have been taken into account and to apportion time, whether extended or reduced, specifically against individual events or omissions.

If the details necessary to describe adequately the Relevant Events or Relevant Omissions cannot be accommodated on the printed form, they should be given on a clearly identified sheet to be firmly attached and referred to on the form.

Make the appropriate deletions depending on the circumstances relating to the notice (i.e. whether it is one which is issued in respect of an extension, reduction or confirmation of the existing) and whether it is in respect of circumstances during the contract or upon review.

Notification of Extension of Time

Issued by: Ivor Barch Associates
address: Prospects Drive, Fairbridge

Employer: Cosmeston Prep School
address: Fairbridge

Contractor: L&M Construction Ltd
address: Ferry Road, Fairbridge

Works situated at: New School Library
Park Street, Fairbridge

Contract dated: 7 December 2011

Job reference: IBA/05/20
Notification no: 6
Issue date: 5 January 2013

SBC

Under the terms of the above-mentioned Contract, this is notification that the Completion Date for

Delete as appropriate

* the Works
* ~~Section no. _____ of the Works~~

previously fixed as
17 November 20 12

* is hereby fixed later than that previously fixed,
* ~~is hereby fixed earlier than that previously fixed,~~
* ~~is hereby confirmed,~~

and is now
19 January 20 13

* The extension of time attributed to each Relevant Event is as follows:

   2.29.9 – Exceptionally adverse weather – 5 weeks
   2.29.2 – Architect's Instructions – 4 weeks

* ~~The reduction in time attributed to each Relevant Omission is as follows:~~

* ~~This decision is made by reason of my/our review.~~

To be signed by or for the issuer named above

Signed *Ivor Barch*

Distribution: Contractor, Quantity Surveyor, M&E Consultant, CDM Co-ordinator, Employer, Structural Engineer, Clerk of Works, File

■ **Notification of Extension of Time**

Issue

Send the original to the Contractor and a duplicate to the Employer at the same time. Send copies to the Quantity Surveyor, CDM Co-ordinator if appointed, other consultants and Clerk of Works, as applicable. File an exact copy.

Non-Completion Certificate

Clause 2.31

Use

If the Contractor fails to complete the Works by the Completion Date, the Architect must issue a certificate to that effect.

Where the Works are divided into Sections, if the Contractor fails to complete any Section by the relevant Completion Date, then the Architect must issue a certificate to that effect.

The Completion Date is the Date for Completion of the Works or of a Section, stated in the Contract Particulars or as revised by an adjustment under clause 2.28 or a Pre-Agreed Adjustment referred to by clause 2.26.2. The certificate must be issued before the Employer is entitled to recover liquidated damages under clause 2.32. This certificate will be cancelled by the fixing of a new Completion Date, and a new certificate must be then issued (if relevant).

Completing

The name and address of issuer, Employer and Contractor should correspond with entries in the Articles of Agreement of the Contract. The signature on the certificate should be that of, or on behalf of, the issuer named in Article 3. The location of the Works (an abbreviated entry) and Contract Date provide precise identification, and should correspond with entries in the Articles and Recitals of the Contract. The job reference will be the office reference for the project, and the certificate number should be inserted.

Delete depending on whether non-completion is in respect of the Works or a Section identified in the Contract Particulars.

Enter the original Completion Date as stated in the Contract Particulars, or as subsequently last revised.

Issue

Send the certificate to the Employer and to the Contractor at the same time. Send copies to the Quantity Surveyor, CDM Co-ordinator if appointed, other consultants and Clerk of Works, as applicable. File an exact copy.

Note: The latest date for the issue of this most important document is the date of issue of the Final Certificate, but in view of its factual nature it is suggested that the certificate should be issued immediately the Completion Date has passed.

Non-Completion Certificate

Issued by: Ivor Barch Associates
address: Prospects Drive, Fairbridge

Employer: Cosmeston Prep School
address: Fairbridge

Contractor: L&M Construction Ltd
address: Ferry Road, Fairbridge

Works situated at: New School Library
Park Street, Fairbridge

Contract dated: 7 December 2011

Job reference: IBA/05/20
Certificate no: 1
Issue date: 20 January 2013

Under the terms of the above-mentioned Contract,

I/we hereby certify that the Contractor has failed to complete

*Delete as appropriate

* the Works

* ~~Section no. _____ of the Works~~

by the relevant Completion Date, namely

19 January 20 13

Signed *Ivor Barch*

To be signed by or for the issuer named above

Distribution: Employer, Contractor, Quantity Surveyor, Structural Engineer, M&E Consultant, Clerk of Works, CDM Co-ordinator, File

for SBC / IC / ICD   CONTRACT ADMINISTRATION FORMS   © RIBA Publishing 2011

Practical Completion Certificate

Clause 2.30

Use

When in the opinion of the Architect practical completion of the Works is achieved, this must be certified.

A separate Section Completion Certificate must be issued where the Works are divided into Sections. In such cases, a Section Completion Certificate must be issued in respect of practical completion of the Works for each Section *in addition* to a Practical Completion Certificate for practical completion of the Works as a whole, which must be issued on the same date as the last Section Completion Certificate.

Partial possession by the Employer (under clause 2.33) requires a written notice, but although practical completion is deemed to have occurred for certain purposes, a Practical Completion Certificate is not issued until completion of the Works.

Clause 2.30 includes the proviso 'and the Contractor has complied sufficiently with clauses 2.40 and 3.23.4'. This is a condition precedent to certifying practical completion. By clause 3.23.4, the Contractor is obliged, within the time reasonably required in writing by the CDM Co-ordinator, to pass such information to the CDM Co-ordinator as may be reasonably required for preparation of the health and safety file. Clause 2.40 only applies if there is a Contractor's Designed Portion. It requires the Contractor to have supplied as-built information as specified in the Contract Documents. It is good practice to remind the Contractor of these conditions some weeks before practical completion is expected.

Completing

The name and address of issuer, Employer and Contractor should correspond with entries in the Articles of Agreement of the Contract. The signature on the certificate should be that of, or on behalf of, the issuer named in Article 3. The location of the Works (an abbreviated entry) and Contract Date provide precise identification, and should correspond with the entries in the Articles and Recitals of the Contract. The job reference will be the office reference for the project, and the certificate number will relate to the particular project.

It is suggested that compliance by the Contractor with clause 3.23.4 should first be confirmed in writing by the CDM Co-ordinator.

Issue

Send the certificate to the Employer and to the Contractor at the same time. Send copies to the Quantity Surveyor, CDM Co-ordinator if appointed, other consultants and Clerk of Works, as applicable. File an exact copy.

Note: Take care when entering the date on which practical completion was achieved. It is very important contractually, and might not be the same date as that for issue of the certificate. It is sound practice to note on the file copy the date when the Rectification Period ends.

Practical Completion Certificate

Issued by: Ivor Barch Associates
address: Prospects Drive, Fairbridge

Employer: Cosmeston Prep School
address: Fairbridge

Contractor: L&M Construction Ltd
address: Ferry Road, Fairbridge

Works: New School Library
situated at: Park Street, Fairbridge

Contract dated: 7 December 2011

Job reference: IBA/05/20

Certificate no: 1

Issue date: 26 January 2013

SBC / IC / ICD / MW / MWD

Under the terms of the above-mentioned Contract,

I/we hereby certify that in my/our opinion

practical completion of the Works has been achieved

*Delete if not applicable

* and the Contractor has supplied the specified documents and drawings relating to the Contractor's Designed Portion

* and the Contractor has complied with the contractual requirements in respect of information for the health and safety file

on 26 January 20 13

To be signed by or for the issuer named above

Signed _Ivor Barch_

Distribution

☐ Employer	☐ Structural Engineer	☐ CDM Co-ordinator	☐
☐ Contractor	☐ M&E Consultant	☐	☐
☐ Quantity Surveyor	☐ Clerk of Works	☐	☐ File

for SBC / IC / ICD / MW / MWD   CONTRACT ADMINISTRATION FORMS   © RIBA Publishing 2011

Section Completion Certificate

Clause 2.30

Use

When in the opinion of the Architect practical completion of a Section is achieved, the Architect must issue a certificate of practical completion of that Section. There is a special certificate for that purpose: the Section Completion Certificate. A Section Completion Certificate must be issued for each Section as it achieves practical completion. However, when the last of the Sections is certified in this way the Architect must issue on the same date a Practical Completion Certificate for the whole of the Works. This is for the avoidance of doubt. The Contractor has undertaken to complete the Works. Therefore, it is essential that there is a certificate that 'the Works' have achieved practical completion. The issue of an all-embracing Practical Completion Certificate will also avoid the not uncommon situation where the sum of the Sections does not quite amount to the Works.

If the Architect on behalf of the Employer issues a Notice of Partial Possession for part of a Section (clause 2.33), practical completion is deemed, for specific purposes, to have occurred for that part. However, no certificate is to be issued until practical completion of the whole of that particular Section has been achieved.

The proviso in clause 2.30 that the Contractor has complied sufficiently with clauses 2.40 and 3.23.4 applies to practical completion of each Section as well as to the Works. The Architect is not empowered to certify practical completion of a Section until the Contractor has passed such health and safety information to the CDM Co-ordinator as is reasonably required. If there is a Contractor's Designed Portion, the Contractor must have supplied such as-built information as specified in the Contract Documents. In similar fashion to the preparation for practical completion of the Works, it is good practice for the Architect to remind the Contractor of these conditions a few weeks before practical completion of the Section is envisaged.

Completing

The name and address of issuer, Employer and Contractor should correspond with entries in the Articles of Agreement of the Contract. The signature on the certificate should be that of, or on behalf of, the issuer named in Article 3. The location of the Works (an abbreviated entry) and Contract Date provide precise identification, and should correspond with the entries in the Articles and Recitals of the Contract. The job reference will be the office reference for the project and the certificate number will relate to the particular project (there might be several Sections). Delete as appropriate in regard to the Contractor's Designed Portion and the health and safety file.

It is suggested that compliance by the Contractor with clause 3.23.4 should first be confirmed in writing by the CDM Co-ordinator.

Issue

Send the certificate to the Employer and to the Contractor at the same time. Send copies to the Quantity Surveyor, the CDM Co-ordinator if appointed, other consultants and Clerk of Works, as applicable. File an exact copy.

Note: Take care when entering the date on which Section practical completion was achieved. It is very important contractually, and might not be the same date as that for the issue of the certificate. It is sound practice to note on the file copy the date when the Rectification Period ends.

Section Completion Certificate

Section Completion Certificate

SBC / IC / ICD

Issued by:
address:

Employer:
address:

Contractor:
address:

Works:
situated at:

Contract dated:

Job reference:

Certificate no:

Issue date:

Under the terms of the above-mentioned Contract,

I/we hereby certify that in my/our opinion

practical completion of

Section no. _____ of the Works

has been achieved

*Delete if not applicable

* and the Contractor has supplied the specified drawings and information relating to the Contractor's Designed Portion

* and the Contractor has complied with the contractual requirements in respect of information for the health and safety file

on _____ 20 _____

To be signed by or for the issuer named above

Signed _____

Distribution:
- [ ] Employer
- [ ] Contractor
- [ ] Quantity Surveyor
- [ ] Structural Engineer
- [ ] M&E Consultant
- [ ] Clerk of Works
- [ ] CDM Co-ordinator
- [ ]
- [ ]
- [ ]
- [ ] File

for SBC / IC / ICD   CONTRACT ADMINISTRATION FORMS   © RIBA Publishing 2011

Certificate of Making Good

Clause 2.39

Use

When in the opinion of the Architect the Contractor has completed the obligation to make good defects, this must be certified. This one certificate refers both to defects which were made good during the Rectification Period and to those which were scheduled within 14 days of the end of the Rectification Period. Where the Works are divided into Sections, a separate Rectification Period operates for each Section.

Where clause 2.33 has been implemented and the Employer has taken partial possession, the Rectification Period for the 'Relevant Part' runs from the 'Relevant Date' given in the Notice of Partial Possession on behalf of the Employer. A Certificate of Making Good is required for each of the parts identified in the notice.

Clause 2.38 provides that the Architect may, with the consent of the Employer, instruct that some or all of the defects are *not* to be made good by the Contractor. If no defects are to be made good, then a Certificate of Making Good is obviously not required. Reference in clause 4.15.1.2 to its date of issue in the context of the Final Certificate will not be relevant in this case.

In the event that making good defects is an operation which requires notification to the Health and Safety Executive (HSE) Area Office, this could constitute a separate project. In any case the CDM Co-ordinator should be kept informed of what defects the Contractor is obliged to make good – there could be health and safety implications.

Completing

The name and address of the issuer, Employer and Contractor should correspond with the entries in the Articles of Agreement of the Contract. The signature on the certificate should be that of, or on behalf of, the issuer named in Article 3. The location of the Works (an abbreviated entry) and Contract Date provide precise identification, and should correspond with entries in the Articles and Recitals of the Contract. The job reference will be the office reference for the project, and the certificate number should be inserted.

Make appropriate deletions, depending on whether the certificate refers to the Works, a Section or a relevant part taken into partial possession. Identify the number and date of the certificate or notice which started the Rectification Period.

Issue

Send the certificate to the Employer and to the Contractor at the same time. Send copies to the Quantity Surveyor, CDM Co-ordinator if appointed, other consultants and Clerk of Works, as applicable. File an exact copy.

Note: Take care over the date of issue of this certificate; it may be relevant in the context of the issue of the Final Certificate (see clause 4.15.1.2).

Certificate of Making Good

SBC/IC/ICD

Issued by: Ivor Barch Associates
address: Prospects Drive, Fairbridge

Employer: Cosmeston Prep School
address: Fairbridge

Contractor: L&M Construction Ltd
address: Ferry Road, Fairbridge

Works: New School Library
situated at: Park Street, Fairbridge

Contract dated: 7 December 2011

Job reference: IBA/05/20
Certificate no: 1
Issue date: 1 September 2013

Under the terms of the above-mentioned Contract,

I/we hereby certify that the Contractor's obligation to make good any defects, shrinkages or other faults which have appeared during the Rectification Period and been notified to the Contractor

relating to

Delete as appropriate

* the Works referred to in the Practical Completion Certificate

  no. 1   dated 26 January 2013

~~* Section no. _____ of the Works referred to in the~~
Section Completion Certificate

  no. _____ dated _____

* the part of the Works identified in the Notice of Partial Possession by the Employer

  ~~no. _____ dated _____~~

have in my/our opinion been discharged on

6 September   20 13

To be signed by or for the issuer named above

Signed *Ivor Barch*

Distribution: Employer ☐ Structural Engineer ☐ CDM Co-ordinator ☐ ☐
Contractor ☐ M&E Consultant ☐ ☐
Quantity Surveyor ☐ Clerk of Works ☐ File ☐

for SBC/IC/ICD   CONTRACT ADMINISTRATION FORMS   © RIBA Publishing 2011

Final Certificate

Clause 4.15

Use

The amendments to the Housing Grants, Construction and Regeneration Act 1996 which have been effected as a result of the Local Democracy, Economic Development and Construction Act 2009 have been reflected in changes to the certification and payment provisions of the contract. The Architect must still certify the amount of final payment to be made by the Employer to the Contractor, but other things have changed including the provisions for notices.

The architect must issue a Final Certificate. It must be within 2 months of whichever occurs last of the following:

- end of the Rectification Period of the Works or the last Section;
- issue of Certificate of Making Good or the last such Certificate where applicable;
- date when the Contractor was sent the final account details (computations of the adjusted Contract Sum).

The due date is the date of issue of the Final Certificate. But if the Final Certificate is not issued within the 2-month period, the due date is the last day of that period.

If the Architect fails to issue the Final Certificate in accordance with clause 4.15.1, the Contractor may give a Final Payment Notice to the Employer at any time after the 2-month period noted in clause 4.15.1, stating the sum the Contractor considers became due on the due date and showing the basis on which it has been calculated. It is obviously important that the Architect issues the Final Certificate on time.

The final date for payment is 28 days from the due date. If the Contractor gives a Final Payment Notice, following the Architect's failure to issue a Final Certificate in time, the final date for payment is postponed by the number of days after the expiry of the 2-month period in clause 4.15.1 that the Final Payment Notice was given. The amount to be paid is the amount stated in the Final Certificate or, if no Final Certificate is issued, in the Final Payment Notice, in each case subject to any Pay Less Notice.

Clause 4.15.2 requires that the Final Certificate states the Contract Sum adjusted as necessary and the sum of the amounts stated as due in Interim Certificates together with any advance payment and sums paid in respect of Interim Payment Notices. The final payment is the difference between the two sums shown as a balance in favour of the Contractor or the Employer. The basis on which the amount was calculated must be stated. This requirement might be met by attaching a copy, or a brief summary, of the final account.

An Employer who wishes to pay less than the amount stated as due in the Final Certificate or in the Final Payment Notice, must give a Pay Less Notice to the Contractor no later than 5 days before the final date for payment.

The Pay Less Notice must state the amount the Employer considers is due and the basis of calculation. It should be noted that a Pay Less Notice may be given on the Employer's behalf by the Architect, Quantity Surveyor or any other person notified to the Contractor as authorised by the Employer to do so. It may not be given until a Final Certificate or a Final Payment Notice has been issued. Note that under clause 4.15.7 interest will become payable if the Employer fails to pay sums properly due within the prescribed period.

Final Certificate

Issued by: Ivor Barch Associates
address: Prospects Drive, Fairbridge

Employer: Cosmeston Prep School
address: Fairbridge

Contractor: L&M Construction Ltd
address: Ferry Road, Fairbridge

Works: New School Library
situated at: Park Street, Fairbridge

Contract dated: 7 December 2011

Job reference: IBA/05/20
Date of issue: 5 October 2013
Due date: 5 October 2013
Final date for payment: 2 November 2013

This Final Certificate is issued under the terms of the above-mentioned Contract.

Contract Sum adjusted in accordance with clause 4.3 (calculation attached)	£ 511,187.00
Sum of amounts already stated as due in Interim Certificates plus amount of any advance payment and payments in respect of any Interim Payment Notices	£ 502,064.00
Difference between the above stated amounts	£ 9,123.00

All amounts are exclusive of VAT. The Employer shall in addition pay the amount of VAT properly chargeable.

I/We hereby certify the sum of (in words)
Nine Thousand One Hundred and Twenty Three pounds only

as a **balance due**:

* Delete as appropriate

* to the Contractor from the Employer.

~~* to the Employer from the Contractor.~~

To be signed by or for the issuer named above

Signed *Ivor Barch*

This is not a Tax Invoice.

| Distribution | ☐ Employer | ☐ Contractor | ☐ Quantity Surveyor | ☐ File copy |

for SBC/IC/ICD   CONTRACT ADMINISTRATION FORMS   © RIBA Publishing 2011

■ **Final Certificate**

The Final Certificate is conclusive evidence in respect of the balance due, in respect of extensions of time and reimbursement of direct loss and/or expense and in respect of the reasonable satisfaction of the Architect for particular matters only where these have been made an express requirement in the Contract Documents or an Architect's Instruction. It is *not* conclusive evidence that the Contractor has complied with the terms of the Contract in respect of materials, goods or workmanship generally (Clause 1.9). However, it should be noted that if the Architect does not issue the Final Certificate in accordance with clause 4.15.1 and the Contractor issues a Final Payment Notice, the result will be that no Final Certificate is issued and, therefore, there will be no conclusive evidence about the matters referred to in this paragraph.

Completing

Enter the name and address of the issuer, Employer and Contractor. Enter the location of the Works (abbreviated) and the Contract Date to give precise identification. Enter the office job reference number. Enter the date of issue of the certificate, and the final date for payment. These are very important in relation to the Contract conditions.

Enter details of payment certified:

- the Contract Sum adjusted in accordance with clause 4.3;
- total amount previously certified, and any advance payment and payments in respect of any Interim Payment Notices;
- the difference between the two amounts;
- whether this balance is due to the Contractor or to the Employer.

Enter the resulting balance due and certified for payment. Entry is to be in figures followed by words. (All these figures are exclusive of VAT.)

The signature on the certificate should be that of, or on behalf of, the issuer named in Article 3.

Issue

Send the certificate to the Employer and to the Contractor at the same time. Remember to attach a statement showing to what the amount relates and how calculated. Send a copy of each to the Quantity Surveyor. File exact copies.

Checklists and References

Checklist 1: Action reminders at pre-contract stage

Recitals and Articles

- [ ] CHECK that drawings and bills/specification/schedules of work are those which are supplied for tendering purposes. If not, deal with implications of changes.

  (SBC/XQ has no bills of quantities)

- [ ] CHECK that the Contractor has supplied fully priced copy of bills/specification/schedules of work, and a priced Activity Schedule if required.

  (SBC/XQ has no bills of quantities)

- [ ] CHECK that Contract Drawings are each identified by number, listed, and signed by the parties.

- [ ] CHECK that the Information Release Schedule is agreed and ready for the Contractor (delete if this item is not required, and note consequential changes to the Contract conditions).

- [ ] CHECK whether Sections and/or Contractor's Designed Portion will be required, and amend the Recitals accordingly.

- [ ] CHECK whether the Architect is also to act as CDM Co-ordinator, and, if not, establish identity of that person.

- [ ] CHECK that the Contractor has prepared a suitable Construction Phase Plan to allow work to start.

Contract Particulars Entries

- [ ] CHECK dates for possession and completion for the Works or for Sections if applicable.
- [ ] CHECK whether deferment of possession is to apply. If so, enter the period.
- [ ] CHECK if a Framework Agreement is involved.
- [ ] CHECK which, if any, of the Supplemental Provisions are to apply and the names of nominees under paragraph 6.
- [ ] CHECK that a Base Date has been entered.
- [ ] CHECK addresses for service of notices.
- [ ] CHECK if critical path is required in master programme.
- [ ] CHECK rate or rates of liquidated damages with the Employer.
- [ ] CHECK duration of the Rectification Period.
- [ ] CHECK that the Employer has taken expert advice regarding insurance then:
  - [ ] CHECK on minimum insurance cover for indemnity under clause 6.4.1.2.
  - [ ] CHECK whether, under clause 6.5, special Employer's liability insurance for property other than the Works is required. If so, make appropriate entry accordingly.
  - [ ] CHECK who is to insure the Works. Whichever clause is to apply, state the percentage to cover professional fees and include for CDM Co-ordinator where applicable.
  - [ ] CHECK whether the Joint Fire Code is to apply.

■ Checklists

- [ ] CHECK what terrorism cover is required.
- [ ] CHECK entries for CDP and amount of indemnity for Professional Indemnity (PI) insurance cover under clause 6.12.
- [ ] CHECK if Employer wishes to assign rights under clause 7.2.
- [ ] CHECK if advance payment is to be made, when and to what sum and the amount and frequency of repayment.
- [ ] CHECK if Employer is prepared to pay for off-site materials.
- [ ] CHECK the Retention percentage.
- [ ] CHECK with the Employer whether bonds are required in respect of Advance Payment, off-site materials and/or goods and Retention.
- [ ] CHECK fluctuation clause required.
- [ ] CHECK whether Adjudicator is to be named in contract. If so, investigate a suitable person. In any event, identify the nominating body.
- [ ] CHECK whether final resolution of disputes is to be by arbitration. If so, make the relevant deletion and identify the appointing body.
- [ ] CHECK whether third party rights or warranties are required from the Contractor, or warranties from sub-contractors.

Attestation

- [ ] CHECK whether the Contract is to be executed under hand or as a deed. In local authority versions, check the attestation requirement.
- [ ] CHECK that the date entered as the date the Agreement was made is the date on which the last party executed the Contract.

Conditions

Clause 2.7

- [ ] CHECK whether there is to be work not forming part of the Contract. Describe in the Contract Documents, if possible.

Clause 2.9.2

- [ ] CHECK what details are required to be included in the Contractor's master programme.

Clause 2.9.5

- [ ] CHECK whether any amendments are required to the Contractor's Design Submission Procedure and advise Employer to have them drafted and included in the Contract Documents.

Clause 2.13

- [ ] CHECK whether there are billed items which do not comply with Standard Method of Measurement (SMM) Rules. If so, identify.

(SBC/XQ has no bills of quantities)

Clause 2.21

- [ ] CHECK whether royalties, if applicable, have been included in the Contract Sum.

Clause 3.3

- [ ] CHECK whether the Employer intends to appoint a representative.

Clause 3.4

- [ ] CHECK whether the Employer intends to appoint a clerk of works.

Clause 3.8

☐ CHECK that where the Contractor is required to sub-let to firms from a given list, such work is properly measured or described in the Contract.

Clause 3.17

☐ CHECK if there is to be provision for testing in the Contract Documents. If so, include provisional sum item.

Clauses 4.6 to 4.13

☐ CHECK on the dates for Interim Certificates, and that the Employer is aware of the requirements concerning written notices, and of obligations concerning payments of amounts certified and the payment of VAT.

Clause 4.17

☐ CHECK whether the Employer intends any off-site materials to be 'Listed Items'.

Clause 5.1.2

☐ CHECK whether there are to be restrictions imposed on access to site, working space, working hours or execution of work in any specific order. Describe in the Contract Documents.

Checklist 2: Architect's duties (SHALL) and empowered discretionary actions (MAY) during work on site

The architect –

Clause 1.7.1

SHALL issue instructions in writing.

Clause 1.8

SHALL issue certificates to the Employer and to the Contractor at the same time.

Clause 2.2.2

SHALL issue directions regarding integration of CDP with the design of the Works.

Clause 2.3.4

MAY request the Contractor to provide reasonable proof that materials or goods comply with the standards of the contract.

Clause 2.8

SHALL provide certified copy of Contract Documents to the Contractor.

SHALL provide two further copies of Contract Drawings and unpriced bills (*specification/schedules of work*).

Clause 2.9.1.1

SHALL provide descriptive schedules or other such documents to the Contractor.

Clause 2.10

SHALL determine levels and provide accurately dimensioned drawings for setting out the Works.

MAY instruct that errors arising from Contractor's inaccurate setting out not be amended and a deduction made from the Contract Sum.

Clause 2.11

SHALL ensure that information is released to the Contractor at dates scheduled on the Information Release Schedule (where applicable).

Checklists

Clause 2.12

SHALL provide further necessary drawings or details to the Contractor.

Clauses 2.15 and 2.16

SHALL issue instructions to the Contractor where discrepancies in or divergence between documents is reported.

Clause 2.16.2

MAY agree amendment after discrepancy found in CDP documents.

Clause 2.17

SHALL issue instructions to the Contractor where divergence between statutory requirements and information provided, is reported.

Clause 2.24

MAY consent to the removal of unfixed goods or materials.

Clause 2.28

SHALL give in writing a fair and reasonable extension of time, if appropriate, in response to written notice by the Contractor or notify Contractor that no extension is given.

Clause 2.28.4

MAY, after the first extension is given, reduce extension to take account of omissions.

Clause 2.28.5

SHALL, not later than 12 weeks after practical completion, review Completion Date or Dates and confirm or amend it (them).

Clause 2.30

SHALL issue a Practical Completion Certificate for the Works in addition to any certificates issued previously relating to Section completion. This certificate also signifies sufficient compliance with the requirement to provide health and safety file information and, where CDP is involved, the as-built information.

SHALL issue a Section Completion Certificate for each Section. This certificate also signifies sufficient compliance of each Section with the requirement to provide health and safety file information and, where CDP is involved, the as-built information.

Clause 2.31

SHALL issue a Non-Completion Certificate of the Works or Section where applicable, and issue a further certificate if circumstances so require.

Clause 2.33

SHALL issue a written notice confirming partial possession of any part of the Works by the Employer.

Clause 2.35

SHALL issue a Certificate of Making Good in respect of the Relevant Part taken into partial possession.

Clause 2.38.1

SHALL, where applicable, prepare a schedule of defects at the end of the Rectification Period and issue it to the Contractor not later than 14 days after expiry of that period.

Clause 2.38.2

MAY issue instructions for defects to be made good, but not after the issue of the schedule of defects or 14 days after the expiry of the Rectification Period.

MAY, with the Employer's consent, instruct that defects are not to be made good.

Clause 2.39

SHALL, where applicable, issue a Certificate of Making Good in respect of the Works and any Section.

Clause 3.1

MAY authorise a person to have right of access to workshops and premises.

Clause 3.7

MAY give consent in writing to sub-contract work or, if relevant, CDP design.

Clause 3.11

MAY issue notice to the Contractor to comply with instructions.

Clause 3.12

MAY confirm instructions in writing. Instructions other than in writing are to be of no immediate effect until confirmed in writing.

Clause 3.13

SHALL specify in writing the authority for issuing instructions if requested to do so by the Contractor.

Clause 3.14

MAY issue instructions to vary the Works or restrictions imposed on the Contractor by the Employer or, in the case of CDP work, to vary the Employer's Requirements.

MAY sanction in writing any variation made by the Contractor (3.14.4).

Clause 3.15

MAY issue instructions to postpone work.

Clause 3.16

SHALL issue instructions about provisional sums.

Clause 3.17

MAY issue instructions on testing or inspection of work or materials.

Clause 3.18

MAY issue instructions requiring removal of work and materials from the site (3.18.1).

MAY allow work not in accordance with the Contract to remain, subject to consultation with the Contractor and the agreement of the Employer (3.18.2).

MAY issue instructions for variations necessary after a clause 3.18.1 instruction (3.18.3).

MAY issue instructions for further tests or opening up following discovery of non-compliance (3.18.4).

Clause 3.19

MAY issue instructions where work is not carried out in a proper and workmanlike manner, or is not in accordance with the Construction Phase Plan.

■ Checklists

Clause 3.20

SHALL give reasons for dissatisfaction within a reasonable time of the execution of unsatisfactory work.

Clause 3.21

MAY issue instructions requiring the exclusion of any person from the site.

Clause 3.22.2

SHALL issue instructions if antiquities are found.

Clause 4.5.2.1

SHALL, unless already ascertained, ascertain loss and/or expense or instruct the Quantity Surveyor to do so.

Clause 4.5.2

SHALL send to the Contractor a copy of the final account.

Clause 4.10.1

SHALL issue Interim Certificates no later than 5 days after each due date.

Clause 4.13.1.1

MAY give a Pay Less Notice on behalf of the Employer.

Clause 4.14

SHALL deal with applications for costs and expenses following suspension.

Clause 4.15.1

SHALL issue the Final Certificate within 2 months of sending the final account to the Contractor, or of the end of the Rectification Period, or of the issue of the Certificate of Making Good.

Clause 4.18.2

SHALL prepare or instruct the Quantity Surveyor to prepare a statement of the amount of Retention deducted.

Clause 4.19.1

SHALL, where there is a Retention Bond, prepare or instruct the Quantity Surveyor to prepare a statement of the amount of Retention which would have been deducted.

Clause 4.23

SHALL ascertain, or instruct the QS to ascertain, loss and expense because regular progress of the Works or part thereof has been materially affected by deferment or one of the Relevant Matters.

Clause 5.3.1

MAY, in an instruction for a variation, request the Contractor to provide a quotation.

Clause 5.3.2

MAY give a further instruction that the variation is to be carried out and valued by Valuation.

Clause 6.5

SHALL, where requested, instruct the Contractor to take out a joint names policy for the amount of indemnity in the Contract Particulars. See that policies and receipts are deposited with the Employer before work starts on site and that the Employer is advised to obtain specialist insurance advice about the adequacy of such policies. Check continuity of cover at appropriate intervals.

Clause 6.12.3

MAY reasonably request the Contractor to produce evidence of CDP Professional Indemnity Insurance.

Clause 6.16.2

SHALL issue any necessary instructions to the extent that Remedial Measures require a variation.

Clause 8.4.1

MAY give notice to the Contractor specifying default which could result in the Employer giving a termination notice to the Contractor.

Clause 8.7.4

SHALL issue a certificate setting out an account of termination costs if the Employer does not send a statement to that effect.

Schedule 1, para 1

MAY agree that the Contractor shall not submit two copies of the Contractor's Design Documents.

Schedule 1, para 2

SHALL return copy of Contractor's Design Document marked 'A', 'B' or 'C' with comments as appropriate.

Schedule 1, para 7

SHALL, within 7 days of receipt of Contractor's notice, confirm or withdraw a comment on the Contractor's design documents.

Schedule 2, para 1

SHALL provide information reasonably required by the Contractor (para 1.1).

Schedule 2, para 2

SHALL invite the Contractor's proposals if acceleration required (para 2.1).

Schedule 2, para 4

SHALL confirm acceptance by the Employer of Variation or Acceleration Quotation where applicable.

Schedule 2, para 5

SHALL give instructions on variation if the Employer does not accept Schedule 2 Quotation (para 5.1).

Schedule 3, para A.2

SHALL check that the Contractor deposits policies and receipts for cover required under Option A for transmission to Employer before work starts, and that the Employer is advised to obtain specialist insurance advice about the adequacy of such policies. Check continuity of cover at appropriate intervals. Joint names policies should provide for recognition of sub-contractors or a waiver of subrogation (the right of an insurer who compensates a policy holder for loss to stand in the shoes and recover from the person who caused the loss).

Schedule 3, paras B.3.5 and C.4.5.2

SHALL treat loss or damage affecting the Works restoration, replacement or repair as a variation to be valued under section 5.

References

All documents listed are available from RIBA bookshops or from RIBA Publications (see page 2).

JCT contracts and related documents

Standard Building Contract (SBC11)

in three versions

With Quantities (SBC11/Q)

With Approximate Quantities (SBC11/AQ)

Without Quantities (SBC11/XQ)

Sub-Contract documents

SBCSub/D/A	Standard Building Sub-Contract with sub-contractor's design Agreement
SBCSub/D/C	Standard Building Sub-Contract with sub-contractor's design Conditions
SBCSub/A	Standard Building Sub-Contract Agreement
SBCSub/C	Standard Building Sub-Contract Conditions

Guides

Guide to SBC11, Sarah Lupton, RIBA Publishing, 2011.

Contract administration forms for SBC11

Clerk of Works Direction (by Institute of Clerks of Works)

Architect's Instruction

Instruction continuation sheet

Contract Administrator's Instruction

Interim Certificate

Statement of Retention

Statement of Reimbursement

Notice of Partial Possession by the Employer

Notification of Extension of Time

Non-Completion Certificate

Practical Completion Certificate

Section Completion Certificate

Certificate of Making Good

Final Certificate